First World War
and Army of Occupation
War Diary
France, Belgium and Germany

38 DIVISION
Divisional Troops
Welsh Regiment
19th Battalion Pioneers
5 December 1915 - 30 April 1919

WO95/2548/2

The Naval & Military Press Ltd
www.nmarchive.com
Published in association with The National Archives

Published by

The Naval & Military Press Ltd

Unit 10 Ridgewood Industrial Park,

Uckfield, East Sussex,

TN22 5QE England

Tel: +44 (0) 1825 749494

www.naval-military-press.com

www.nmarchive.com

This diary has been reprinted in facsimile from the original. Any imperfections are inevitably reproduced and the quality may fall short of modern type and cartographic standards.

© **Crown Copyright**
Images reproduced by permission of The National Archives, London, England, 2015.

Contents

Document type	Place/Title	Date From	Date To
Heading	WO95/2548/2		
Heading	38th Division 19th Bn Welsh Regt. (Pioneers) Dec 1915-Apr 1919		
Heading	WO95/2548		
Heading	38th Div 19th Welsh Regt Vol 1 Dec 1915		
War Diary	Boulogne Rest Camp	05/12/1915	05/12/1915
War Diary	Blendecques	06/12/1915	06/12/1915
War Diary	Quistede	06/12/1915	19/12/1915
War Diary	Cornet Malo	20/12/1915	31/12/1915
Heading	19th Welsh Rgt Vol: 2 January 16		
War Diary	Hinges	01/01/1916	22/01/1916
War Diary	Lacouture	23/01/1916	16/02/1916
War Diary	Essars	17/02/1916	29/02/1916
Heading	19th Welsh Reg Vol 4 March 16		
War Diary	Essars	01/03/1916	14/04/1916
War Diary	V.6.d	15/04/1916	16/04/1916
War Diary	Laventie	17/04/1916	11/06/1916
War Diary	Callone Sur La Lys	12/06/1916	13/06/1916
War Diary	Divion	14/06/1916	14/06/1916
War Diary	Villers Chatel.	15/06/1916	25/06/1916
War Diary	Bouquemaison	26/06/1916	27/06/1916
War Diary	Candas	28/06/1916	30/06/1916
Heading	Pioneers. 38th Div. War Diary 19th Battn. The Welch Regiment. July 1916		
War Diary	Inchy	01/07/1916	08/07/1916
War Diary	Mametz Wood	09/07/1916	13/07/1916
War Diary	Longpre	13/07/1916	13/07/1916
War Diary	Gorenflos.	14/07/1916	17/07/1916
War Diary	Sailly Aux Bois.	18/07/1916	31/07/1916
War Diary	Houtkerque	01/08/1916	01/08/1916
War Diary	F Camp. A.16.C.	02/08/1916	12/08/1916
War Diary	F. Camp.	13/08/1916	13/09/1916
War Diary	Welsh Farm	14/09/1916	31/10/1916
War Diary	Ypres Salient	01/11/1916	01/12/1916
War Diary	J. Camp.	02/12/1916	03/12/1916
War Diary	Houlle	04/12/1916	05/01/1917
War Diary	Quelmes	06/01/1917	13/01/1917
War Diary	Ypres. Salient.	14/01/1917	30/06/1917
War Diary	Proven	01/07/1917	19/07/1917
War Diary	Ypres Salient	20/07/1917	28/07/1917
War Diary	X. Day	29/07/1917	29/07/1917
War Diary	Y Day	30/07/1917	30/07/1917
War Diary	Z Day	31/07/1917	31/07/1917
War Diary	Ypres Salient	31/07/1917	03/08/1917
War Diary	Ypres. A.18.a.	04/08/1917	14/08/1917
War Diary	Prove Area	15/08/1917	21/08/1917
War Diary	Ypres Area	21/08/1917	09/09/1917
War Diary	Proven	09/09/1917	13/09/1917
War Diary	Bac St Maur	14/09/1917	18/09/1917
War Diary	Bac St Maur Sheet 36 1/40,000	19/09/1917	29/09/1917

Type	Location/Description	Start	End
War Diary	Bac St Maur.	01/10/1917	18/10/1917
War Diary	Sailly.	19/10/1917	12/11/1917
War Diary	Sailly Sur La Lys	13/11/1917	30/11/1917
War Diary	H.Q. at. Sailly Sur La Lys.	01/12/1917	19/01/1918
War Diary	H.Q at Nouveau Monde	20/01/1918	22/02/1918
War Diary	H.Q at Erquinghem	22/02/1918	28/03/1918
War Diary	Armentieres	29/03/1918	31/03/1918
War Diary	Caudescure	01/04/1918	04/04/1918
War Diary	Warloy	05/04/1918	11/04/1918
War Diary	Senlis	12/04/1918	24/04/1918
War Diary	Herissart	25/04/1918	25/04/1918
War Diary	Senlis	26/04/1918	26/04/1918
War Diary	Herissart	27/04/1918	30/04/1918
Miscellaneous	38th. Division No. S.S. 125/6	26/04/1918	26/04/1918
War Diary	Senlis	01/05/1918	20/05/1918
War Diary	Herissart	21/05/1918	03/06/1918
War Diary	Englebelmer	04/06/1918	30/06/1918
War Diary	Mesnil Sector	01/07/1918	17/07/1918
War Diary	Herissart	18/07/1918	16/08/1918
War Diary	H.Q at V.3. Central	17/08/1918	25/08/1918
War Diary	Bouzincourt	26/08/1918	26/08/1918
War Diary	Bazentin Le Petit.	27/08/1918	31/08/1918
Miscellaneous	19th. Welsh Regt (Pioneers) Operation Order.	23/08/1918	23/08/1918
War Diary	Bazentin Le Petit.	01/09/1918	02/09/1918
War Diary	Morval	03/09/1918	04/09/1918
War Diary	Le Transloy.	05/09/1918	10/09/1918
War Diary	Etricourt	11/09/1918	29/09/1918
War Diary	Heudecourt	30/09/1918	30/09/1918
Operation(al) Order(s)	Battalion Orders 624. by Major R.B. Harkness	03/09/1918	03/09/1918
Miscellaneous	Operation Order By Lieut. Col. D. Grant-Dalton, D.S.O.,	17/09/1918	17/09/1918
Operation(al) Order(s)	Battalion Orders 638. By Lieut. Col. D. Grant-Dalton, D.S.O.,	30/09/1918	30/09/1918
War Diary	Heudicourt	01/10/1918	05/10/1918
War Diary	Epehy	05/10/1918	07/10/1918
War Diary	Vendhuille	08/10/1918	09/10/1918
War Diary	Malincourt	10/10/1918	12/10/1918
War Diary	Bertry	13/10/1918	24/10/1918
War Diary	Montay	25/10/1918	25/10/1918
War Diary	Caluyaux	26/10/1918	31/10/1918
Miscellaneous	Special Order Of The Day by Major General T. Astley Cubitt, CMG., DSO., Commanding 38th. (Welsh) Division.	26/10/1918	26/10/1918
Miscellaneous	Special Order By Lieut. Col. R.B. Harkness, Commanding 19th Welsh Regt.	21/10/1918	21/10/1918
War Diary	Caluyaux	01/11/1918	04/11/1918
War Diary	Englefontaine	05/11/1918	07/11/1918
War Diary	Berlaimont	08/11/1918	09/11/1918
War Diary	Aulnoye	10/11/1918	10/11/1918
War Diary	Ecuelin	11/11/1918	17/11/1918
War Diary	Berlaimont	18/11/1918	30/11/1918
Miscellaneous	O.C. 19th. Welsh Regt. (Glamorgan Pioneers)	16/11/1918	16/11/1918
War Diary	Corbie	01/12/1918	14/12/1918
War Diary	St. Gratien	15/12/1918	02/01/1919
War Diary	La Neuville	03/01/1919	31/01/1919
War Diary	La Neuville Somme	01/02/1919	28/02/1919

War Diary	La Neuville Corbie	01/03/1919	27/03/1919
War Diary	Blangy Tronville.	29/03/1919	31/03/1919
Miscellaneous	38th Div	15/05/1919	15/05/1919
War Diary	Blangy-Tronville.	01/04/1919	30/04/1919

W095/25482

38TH DIVISION

19TH BN WELSH REGT.
(PIONEERS)
DEC 1915-APR 1919

WO 95/2548

19th Welsh Regt.
Vol I
Dec 1915

38th/13

Army Form C. 2118

WAR DIARY
or
INTELLIGENCE SUMMARY
(Erase heading not required.)

19 Pioneers WELSH Regt

Place	Date	Hour	Summary of Events and Information	Remarks and references to Appendices
BOULOGNE Rest Camp.	Dec 5.12.15	2 pm – 8 pm	Rest after debarkation. Recd rations O.D.T.S.	
BLENRECQUES	6	6 am	Detrained. O.D.T.S.	
QUIESTEDE	do	7.30 am	Went into billets. O.D.T.S.	
do	do	11 am	Billeted. O.D.T.S.	
do	7.	All day	Inspection of Wagons. 1 Offr. 50 other ranks proceeded to LA MOTTE for wood cutting. O.D.T.S	
do	8	All day	Training etc. O.D.T.S.	
do	9	All day	Training etc. O.D.T.S.	
do	10	do	do	O.D.T.S.
do	11	"	do	O.D.T.S.
do	12	"	do	O.D.T.S.
do	13	"	do	O.D.T.S.
do	14	"	do	O.D.T.S.
do	15	"	do	O.D.T.S.
do	16	"	B Coy. proceeded to LEVANTIE attached Guards Pioneers	O.D.T.S.
do	17	"	C. Coy. proceeded to Le Touret. O.D.T.S.	
do	18	"	A Coy. & A. Coy. proceeded to LEVANTIE attached Guards Pioneers B. Coy. returned to QUIESTEDE	O.D.T.S.

O.D.T. Clark H.T. Adj.
for C.O. 19th ..

H.Q. Cos. 19TH (PIONEER) BATTALION
JAN 2 1916

Army Form C. 2118

WAR DIARY
or
INTELLIGENCE SUMMARY 19. Pioneers WELSH Regt.
(Erase heading not required.)

Instructions regarding War Diaries and Intelligence Summaries are contained in F. S. Regs., Part II. and the Staff Manual respectively. Title Pages will be prepared in manuscript.

Place	Date	Hour	Summary of Events and Information	Remarks and references to Appendices
QUIESTEDE	19	All day	Training etc. —	
CORNET MALO	20	" "	d.o	O.D.T.B
"	21	" "	d.o	O.D.T.B
"	22	" "	d.o	O.D.T.B
"	23	" "	d.o	O.D.T.B
"	24	" "	d.o D. Coy proceeded to Richebourg. Batt: detachment moved CORNET MALO	O.D.T.B
"	25	" "	d.o	O.D.T.B
"	26	" "	d.o C. Coy returned to Batt. at CORNET MALO	O.D.T.B
"	27	" "	d.o A. Coy and HQrs " " " C. Coy proceeded to LAVENTIE	DppTB
"	28	" "	d.o	O.D.T.B
"	29	" "	d.o	O.D.T.B
"	30	" "	d.o Battn moved to LA PANNERIE	O.D.T.B
"	31	" "	d.o	O.D.T.B

O.D. Black Capt.
pro OC 19th Welsh

19th Welsh Bn.
Vol: 2
Jaury 16

L. F.

Army Form C. 2118

WAR DIARY
or
INTELLIGENCE SUMMARY   19th PIONEERS WELSH REGT.
(Erase heading not required.)

Place	Date	Hour	Summary of Events and Information	Remarks and references to Appendices
HINGES	1.1.16	All day	Training –	OO78
"	2	"	do	OO78
"	3	"	do	OO78
"	4	"	do	O.D.R.
"	5	"	do. D. Coy returned from LACOUTURE – 1.0 p.m.	O.O.78
"	6	"	do.	OO78
"	7	"	do. Casualties 1 killed (C.Coy)	OO78
"	8	"	do. C. Coy returned from LAVENTIE. A. Coy proceeded to LAVENTIE	OO78
"	9	"	do	OO78
"	10	"	do	OO78
"	11	"	do	OO78
"	12	"	do Woodcutting Party LA MOTTE relieved by another party from B. Coy –	OO78
"	13	"	do	OO78
"	14	"	do	OO78
"	15	"	do Major FENNELL proceeded to ENGLAND recalled by W.O	OO78
"	16	"	do	OO78
"	17	"	do	OO78

Army Form C. 2118

WAR DIARY or INTELLIGENCE SUMMARY 19TH PIONEER BATTN WELSH REGT

(Erase heading not required.)

Place	Date	Hour	Summary of Events and Information	Remarks and references to Appendices
HINGES.	18	July	TRAINING.	0748.
	19	"	Do	0748
	20	"	Do	0748
	21	"	Do	0748
	22	"	10.30 Proceeded to LACOUTURE B.Coy - D.Coy & H⁰ Qrs - C.Coy to BOUT DEVILLE -	0748.
LACOUTURE	23	"	Arranging details of work on trenches etc - A.Coy returned - 1 wounded -	0773
	24	"	Work commenced on trenches etc under C.R.E. C.Coy "Draining"	0773
	25	"	Work continued " " " " " " "	0773
	26	"	Do " " " " " " "	0773
	27	"	Do " " " " " " "	0773
	28	"	Do " " " " " " "	0773
	29	"	Do " " " " " " "	0773
	30	"	Do " " " " " " "	0773
	31	"	Battalion Rest Day -	0773

WAR DIARY
or
INTELLIGENCE SUMMARY 19TH PIONEER BATTN WELSH REGT

Army Form C. 2118

(Erase heading not required.)

Instructions regarding War Diaries and Intelligence Summaries are contained in F. S. Regs., Part II. and the Staff Manual respectively. Title Pages will be prepared in manuscript.

Place	Date	Hour	Summary of Events and Information	Remarks and references to Appendices
LACOUTURE	1. FEB. 1916.		Work on trenches and drainage continued.	O.D.73.
	2.	All day	Do. do. Lieut. MEREDITH appointed Quarry Offr - proceeded to HINGES.	D.O.73.
	3.	"	Do. do.	O.D.73
	4.	"	Do. do. Received notification that 2nd Lieut L.S. THOMAS was invalided to ENGLAND 26.1.16. One man wounded - shrapnel.	O.D.73.
	5.	"	Do. do.	O.D.73.
	6.	"	Do. do. One man wounded - rifle bullet. Stretcher bearers 5.30 am	O.D.73.
	7.	"	Do. do.	O.D.73.
	8.	"	Batt. Rest Day. Inspections.	O.D.73.
	9.	"	Do. Major R. LLOYD GEORGE TO hospital (Pyorrhœa).	O.D.73.
	10.	"	Do.	O.D.73.
	11.	"	Do.	O.D.73.
	12.	"	Do. One man wounded - rifle bullet.	O.D.73.
	13.	"	Do. " " " " " 2nd Lt. JAMES HERBERT JENKINS and 27 O.R. joined unit	O.D.73
	14.	"	Do. C. of E. Service for Battn.	O.D.73.

O.D. Black O.C.
19

Army Form C. 2118

WAR DIARY
or
INTELLIGENCE SUMMARY 19TH PIONEER BATTN WELSH REGT.
(Erase heading not required.)

Instructions regarding War Diaries and Intelligence Summaries are contained in F.S. Regs, Part II. and the Staff Manual respectively. Title Pages will be prepared in manuscript.

Place	Date	Hour	Summary of Events and Information	Remarks and references to Appendices
LACOUTURE	15TH	ALL DAY.	Bn Rest Day. - for 3 Coys - C. Coy carried on Drainage Work - after, Inspection -	O.M.13.
	16	"	Work on Trenches not resumed - preparations made for move.	O.N.13.
	17	"	A. B. D. Coys. & H.Q. Coy. moved to ESSARS.	O.O.13.
	18	"	Cleaning billets. Mining party commenced work. C. Coy moves to LACOUTURE	O.M.13.
ESSARS.	19	"	do do Mining work continued. C. Coy carried on drainage work	O.P.13.
	20	"	do do do Bn. 2nd Lt. JOHN BRADFORD joined unit -	O.M.13.
	21	"	do do do Do 3 men wounded (mine explosion)	O.R.13.
	22	"	do do do Do 2 men wounded (rifle grenade)	O.S.13.
	23	"	do do do Do Maj R LLOYD GEORGE returned Do 2 " " (rifle bullets)	O.T.13.
	24	"	do do do Do " "	O.U.13.
	25	"	do do do Do Casualties Nil	O.V.13.
	26	"	do do do Do "	O.W.13.
	27	"	do do do Do 2 men wounded (bullet)	O.X.13.
	28	"	do do do Do 2nd Lt. MATTHEW PETER McDONOUGH joined unit.	O.Y.13.
	29	"	do do do Do Church Service 7.30	O.Z.13.

C.A. Black Maj

38

19th Weld Reg

Vol 4
March 16

H. 7
5 sheets

Army Form C. 2118

WAR DIARY
or
INTELLIGENCE SUMMARY 19th PIONEER BATTN WELSH REGT
(Erase heading not required.)

Place	Date 1916	Hour	Summary of Events and Information	Remarks and references to Appendices
ESSARS	1st MARCH	ALL DAY	Mining Fatigue continued. C. Coy carried on drainage work.	Appx 72
	2nd	do	do	Appx 73
	3rd	do	do	C.O. Lt Col Wilmson on leave to ENGLAND	Appx 73
	4th	do	do		Appx 73
	5th	do	do		Appx 73
	6th	do	do		Appx 73
	7th	do	do	2. Offrs 168 O.R. from 114th Bde attached for mining fatigue	Appx 73
	8th	do	do	A. Coy relieved – rested	Appx 73
	9th	do	do	A. Coy commenced wiring second line	Appx 73
	10th	do	do	A Coy continued wiring	Appx 73
	11th	do	do	do	Appx 73
	12th	do	do	do 2 Offrs 168 O.R. 113th Bde attached	Appx 73
				B. Coy relieved
	13th	do	do	B. Coy rested	Appx 73
	14th	do	do	B. Coy on drainage work	Appx 73

WAR DIARY or INTELLIGENCE SUMMARY 19th PIONEER BATTN WELSH REGT

Army Form C. 2118

(Erase heading not required.)

Place	Date	Hour	Summary of Events and Information	Remarks and references to Appendices
ESSARS	15th	All day	A. Coy. wiring. B and C. Coy. drainage. D. Coy and attached enlist Mining Fatigue.	O.D.T.B
	16th	do	do	O.D.T.B
	17th	do	do	O.D.T.B
	18th	do	do. 50 men attached 258 Tunnelling Coy. 2 Offrs do. 1 man wounded.	O.D.T.B
			A. Coy. wiring. B and C. Coy: drainage. D. Coy attached emit Mining Fatigue.	O.D.T.B
	19th	do	do. C. Coy. red day	O.D.T.B
	20th	do	do. C. Coy drainage. do	O.D.T.B
	21st	do	do. B. Coy. red day. do 1 man wounded (attached)	O.D.T.B
	22nd	do	B. and C. Coy drainage. do	O.D.T.B
	23rd	do	B and C. Coys wiring. D. Coy trench repairs. 2 Offrs and 158 O.R. from 115th Rifle attached for Mining Fatigue. attached Coys Mining Fatigue	O.D.T.B
	24th	do	do	O.D.T.B
	25th	do	do	O.D.T.B
			2nd LT W.T. NEWLYN reports for duty	O.D.T.B

Army Form C. 2118

WAR DIARY
or
INTELLIGENCE SUMMARY 19th PIONEER BATTN. WELSH REGt
(Erase heading not required.)

Instructions regarding War Diaries and Intelligence Summaries are contained in F. S. Regs., Part II. and the Staff Manual respectively. Title Pages will be prepared in manuscript.

Place	Date	Hour	Summary of Events and Information	Remarks and references to Appendices
ESSARS.	MARCH 26	all day	A. Coy - wiring. B and C. drainage. D. Coy trench repair. Attached Coy. Mining	O.O.78.
	27	"	do	O.O.78.
			3 men killed - Lieut. B.J. OWEN & 3 men wounded (shell). Reinforcing draft of 445 men arrived from Base	
	28	"	All Coys and attached working as above.	O.O.78.
	29	"	A. B. & D. Coys - Rest day. Bathing & Kit Inspection. Attached Coys as before. 1 man of attached Coy (grenade).	O.O.78.
	30	"	A. B. & D. Coys fatigues employed as before - C. Coy Rest day. Bathing Kit Inspection. the Qu. Coy. &c.	O.O.78.
	31	"	do. do. C. Coy drainage continued.	O.O.78.

1875 Wt. W593/826 1,000,000 4/15 J.B.C. & A. A.D.S.S./Forms/C. 2118.

Army Form C. 2118

WAR DIARY or INTELLIGENCE SUMMARY

19th PIONEER BATTN WELSH REGT Vol 5

(Erase heading not required.)

Place	Date	Hour	Summary of Events and Information	Remarks and references to Appendices
ESSARS	1916 APRIL 1.	ALL DAY.	A. Coy wiring. Band C. Coys draining D. Coy trench renovating	O.O.73.
	2.	"	Do. do. do. do. attached Coy. Training Fatigue -	O.O.73.
	3.	"	Do. do. do. do. casualties 2 killed 3 wounded. (A Coy. att'd 255 R.E.)	O.O.73.
	4.	"	Do. do. do. do. 1 of yesterday wounded died in Hospital	O.O.73.
	5.	"	Do. do. do. do. 2/Lieut JOHN ELLIOTT SEAGER joined unit	O.O.73.
	6.	"	Do. do. do. do.	O.O.73.
	7.	"	Do. do. do. do. Casualties. 1 wounded.	O.O.73.
	8.	"	Do. do. do. do.	O.O.73.
	9.	"	Do. do. do. do.	O.O.73.
	10.	"	Do. do. do. do.	O.O.73.
	11.	"	Do. do. do. do.	O.O.78.
	12.	"	Do. do. do. do.	O.O.78 E.O.L
	13.	"	Do. do. do. do.	O.O.78
	14.	"	Battalion moved to billets at V.6.d.	O.O.78

Army Form C. 2118

WAR DIARY
or
INTELLIGENCE SUMMARY   19th WELSH
(Erase heading not required.)

Place	Date 4-16	Hour	Summary of Events and Information	Remarks and references to Appendices
V.6.d	15th	allday	Inspections – rest –	O.O.B.
	16	"	Battalion moved to LAVENTIE. Attached Mining Coy moved to LAVENTIE	O.O.B.
LAVENTIE	17	"	Cleaning billets – inspecting work.	O.O.B.
	18	"	A.Coy Entrenching B.Coy draining – C.Coy Mining Fatigue D.Coy Wiring – attached Coy- Mining Fatigue	O.O.B.
	19	"	Do	do	do	do	O.O.B.
	20	"	Do	do	do	do	O.O.B.
	21	"	Do	do	do	do	O.O.B.
	22	"	A.Coy wiring second line trench B.C.D. attached as above –	O.O.B.
	23	"	Do	do	do	O.O.B.
	24	"	Do	do	do 1 wounded / 9th the O.D.S	O.O.B.
			(Major D.GRANT DALTON (11th S.W.B.) assumed comd (2 killed 10th S.W.B. + 1 wounded vice Lt.Col. WILKINSON. transferred. 1 " 11th S.W.B. × 2 " 7am (were from Mining Party attached)	O.O.B.
	25	"	Do	do	O.O.B.

Army Form C. 2118

WAR DIARY
or
INTELLIGENCE SUMMARY
(Erase heading not required.)

19th WELSH

Place	Date	Hour	Summary of Events and Information	Remarks and references to Appendices
LAVENTIE	26th 4.16		A.Coy. wiring B.Coy. draining D.Coy. wiring. C.Coy. out attacks wiring —	O.R.B.
	27		Do. do. 1 killed 2 wounded 19th Welsh	O.R.B.
	28		Do. do. 1 wounded 19th Welsh 1 d. killed.	O.R.B.
	29		Do. do. C.Coy. 25 all ranks making M.G. emplacements	O.R.B.
		10.44	20. O.R. B.Coy drawing in outcrop — 2 wounded 19th Welsh (one mine raid of grenades)	O.R.B.
	30th		Do. do. 40. O.R. of B.Coy. attached to Mining Party	O.R.B.

(Lieut B.J. OWEN evacuated to England out of strength 15.4.16
" L.S. THOMAS. rejoined from England (Hospital) 24.4.16) O.R.B.

Major GEORGE HUGHES EARLE. (11th Hants) joined for duty

[signature]
Major
Comdg 19th Welsh

WAR DIARY or INTELLIGENCE SUMMARY

Army Form C. 2118

XXXVIII 19th Welsh - Vol 6

Place	Date 1916	Hour	Summary of Events and Information	Remarks and references to Appendices
LAVENTIE	MAY 1st		A & D. Coy - wiring. B. Coy. Draining. C. Coy. & attached party from their Sig. Pdn. engaged on Mining Fatigue for 255 Tunnelling Coy. R.E.	07073
	2nd		do. do. do.	07073
	3rd		do. do. do. 1 man killed - bullet. 1 wounded - grenade	07073
	4th		do. do. do. 1 " killed. " 2 wounded - bullet	07073
	5th		do. do. do. C. Coy. 1 section constructing M.G. emplacement.	07073
	6th		do. do. do.	07073
	7th		do. do. do.	07073
	8th		do. do. do. 1 man wounded - bullet. 2/Lt Evan Rees transferred to 255 Tunnelling Coy. R.E.	07073
	9th		do. do. do.	07073
	10th		do. do. do.	07073
	11th		do. do. do.	07073
	12th		do. do. do.	07073
	13th		do. do. do. 1 man wounded - 2/Lt Goronwy Claude Lewis joins unit.	07073
	14th		do. do. do. 1 Sgt. wounded - bullet.	07073

Army Form C. 2118

WAR DIARY or INTELLIGENCE SUMMARY   19th Welsh

(Erase heading not required.)

Place	Date	Hour	Summary of Events and Information	Remarks and references to Appendices
LAYENTIE	15th		At D. Coy. wiring and trench improvement. C. Coy. making M.G. emplacements	O.O.73
	16th		Do. 100 men of C. Coy and attached party on Mining fatigue	O.O.73
	17th		Do. B. Coy. training & trench improvements	O.O.73
	18th		Do.	O.O.73
	19th		Do. 1 wounded. Lieut.	O.O.73
	20th		Do. 1. wounded - at duty (13th R.W.F.) attached	O.O.73
	21st		Do. 2nd Lieut ALFRED MEREDITH proceeded to join 5th Labour Batt. to	O.O.73
	22nd		(1. 14th Welsh 1. 15th Welsh wounded attached) which he was transferred as from 14.4.16.	O.O.73
	23rd		Do. as to work.	O.O.73
	24th		Do. do. to work.	d.o.
	25th		Do. do.	d.o.
	26th		Do. 2nd LIEUT. CHARLES FREDERICK TAYLOR + 1 man wounded (shrapnel)	d.o.
	27th		Do. do.	d.o.

1875 Wt. W593/826 1,000,000 4/15 J.B.C. & A. A.D.S.S./Forms/C. 2118.

Army Form C. 2118

WAR DIARY
or
INTELLIGENCE SUMMARY 19th WELSH.
(Erase heading not required.)

Instructions regarding War Diaries and Intelligence Summaries are contained in F.S. Regs., Part II. and the Staff Manual respectively. Title Pages will be prepared in manuscript.

Place	Date	Hour	Summary of Events and Information	Remarks and references to Appendices
LAVENTIE	28th/5/16		'A' Coy. trench improvements. B Coy. drainage & trench improvements. C Coy. 100 men on mining fatigue & 25 men on M.G. emplacement. D Coy. M.G. emplacement, dugout and trench improvements.	1.D.
	29th		Do. do. do. do. 18 Officers & 520 O.R. 1/5 D.C.L.I. attached for instruction	1.D.
	30		Do. do. do. do.	1.D.
	31st		Do. do. do. do.	1.D.
	1st/6/16		Do. do.	1.D.

Ahmed Dallas Lt Col
Commd 19th Welsh Regt

Army Form C. 2118

June

WAR DIARY or INTELLIGENCE SUMMARY

XXXVII 19th WELSH. VOL 7

(Erase heading not required.)

Instructions regarding War Diaries and Intelligence Summaries are contained in F.S. Regs., Part II. and the Staff Manual respectively. Title Pages will be prepared in manuscript.

Place	Date	Hour	Summary of Events and Information	Remarks and references to Appendices
LAVENTIE	28/5/16		A Coy. Trench improvements. B Coy. drainage & trench improvements. C Coy. 150 men on mining fatigue & 25 men on M.G. emplacement. D Coy. M.G. emplacements	T.P.
	29th		Do. do. do. do. August & Trench emplacements. Attached troops on Mining Fatigue. 18 Officers & 520 O.R. attached for instruction. 1/5 D.C.L.I.	do
	30th		Do. do. do. do.	T.P.
	31st		do. do. do. Lieut C F TAYLOR evacuated to England.	T.P.
	1st/6/16		do do	T.P.
	2nd		do do	OTP
	3rd		do do	OTP
	4th		do do	OTP
	5th		do do	OTP
	6th		do do	OTP
	7th		do do 1 wounded. Shrapnel	OTP
	8th		do do 1 do	OTP
	9th		do do	OTP
	10th		do do	OTP
	11th		do do 2 wounded shell. (one of whom died of wounds)	OTP
			61st Div. relieved 114th Rifle party of Mining Fatigue. D.C.L.I. relieves C Coy.	7.7 3 sheet

Army Form C. 2118

WAR DIARY
or
INTELLIGENCE SUMMARY 19th WELSH
(Erase heading not required.)

Instructions regarding War Diaries and Intelligence Summaries are contained in F.S. Regs., Part II. and the Staff Manual respectively. Title Pages will be prepared in manuscript.

Place	Date	Hour	Summary of Events and Information	Remarks and references to Appendices
CALLONE sur LALYS.	12th 6-16		Batt: left LAVENTIE marched to billets at CALLONE sur LYS. Many fatigue details were returned to their Bttn: from units.	0208
	13th		Battn rested – D.Coy 14th Coy. Fathers.	0208
DIVION	14th		" marched to DIVION in rear of 115 Bde. which billeted at AUCHEL.	0208
VILLERS CHATEL	15th		" " " VILLERS CHATEL and billeted	0208
	16th		" rested and improved billets –	0208
	17th		" commenced training on Area A.	0208
	18th		" Continued Training – 2nd Lt. T. LLEWELYN joined R.F.C. Transferred 18.6.16. 1st Army No 1125/9974 A d. 12.6.16.	0208
	19th		do do	0208
	20th to 23rd		do do	0208
	24th		Continued Company and Battalion Training.	0208
	25th		Rake Training – 1hm B attached 114 Bde. Divisional Training.	0208
BOUQUE MAISON.	26th		Batt: marched to BOUQUEMAISON. arrived 11.0 p.m.	0208
	27th		" " " CANDAS.	0208

Army Form C. 2118

WAR DIARY
or
INTELLIGENCE SUMMARY 19th Welsh

(Erase heading not required.)

Instructions regarding War Diaries and Intelligence Summaries are contained in F. S. Regs., Part II. and the Staff Manual respectively. Title Pages will be prepared in manuscript.

Place	Date	Hour	Summary of Events and Information	Remarks and references to Appendices
CANDAS.	29th	-	Battn rested in billets.	O.O.13.
	29th	-	Inspections —	S.O.13.
	30th	-	Battn marched to Billets VALHEUREUX.	O.O.14.

Thomas Jackson Lt. Col.
o/c 19 Welsh Reg.

Pioneers.
38th Div.

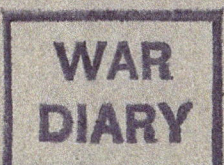

19th BATTN. THE WELCH REGIMENT.

J U L Y

1 9 1 6

INTELLIGENCE SUMMARY

19th WELSH

(Erase heading not required.)

Place	Date	Hour	Summary of Events and Information	Remarks and references to Appendices
July	1st 1916		Battn. marched from VALHEUREUX to camp at PUCHEVILLERS.	A.D.T.S.
	2nd		Battn. parties rested in Camp.	A.D.T.S.
	3rd		Route march en route from 114 Bde. H.Q. Rules afternoon - 7.0 p.m. marched to bivouac at MERICOURT.	A.D.T.S.
	4th		Rested.	A.D.T.S.
	5th		Battn. marched to GROVETOWN CAMP.	A.D.T.S.
	6th		3 Coys marched to MINDEN POST - bivouac on road repairs under C.R.E.'s instructions	A.D.T.S.
	7th		4th Coy & H.Q. moved to MINDEN POST.	A.D.T.S.
	7th		Battn. moved to LOOP TRENCH. waited all day. bivouaced.	A.D.T.S.
	8th		" returned to MINDEN POST. A Coy reports for duty under 113 Bde. - B. Coy attached	A.D.T.S.
			151 Field Coy. - day. took tea at QUEENS NULLAH. C. Coy. employed on Road repairs	A.D.T.S.
MAMETZ WOOD	9th		An afternoon of 9th the Battalion received orders to follow the attack of the Div. on MAMETZ WOOD and consolidate certain points against counter attacks. In accordance with Div. O.O. H.Q. and 2 Coys. were attd. to 114 Inf. Bde. and 2 Coys. to 113 Inf. Bde. & Coys attd. to 114 Bde. tasks were allotted as under: "B" Coy (ees. 1 platoon with 1 sect R.E. to follow attack of 14th Welsh (Left attack of Bde.) Rendezvous night of 9th WHITE TRENCH. H.Q. and C. Coy. 1 Platoon "B" Coy or 151 Coy R.E. bn 1 sect rendezvous night of 9th CATERPILLAR WOOD. 2 Platoons C. Coy. were detailed to enter wood with R.E. behind attack	

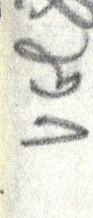

INTELLIGENCE SUMMARY

of 19th WELSH

Instructions regarding War Diaries and Intelligence Summaries are contained in F.S. Regs., Part II. and the Staff Manual respectively. Title Pages will be prepared in manuscript.

(Erase heading not required.)

Place	Date	Hour	Summary of Events and Information	Remarks and references to Appendices
July	9		2 13th Welsh (right attack of Bde.) 2 platoons of "B" Coy. were detailed to dig a C.T. from CATERPILLAR to MAMETZ WOOD. The 1 platoon of "B" Coy. was held as a reserve. All platoons were employed night of 9th to 3.0 a.m. 10th in carrying R.E. material & forming dumps in vicinity of WHITE TRENCH & CATERPILLAR. The 3 platoons "B" Coy. followed the 14th Welsh into the WOOD and were successful in evacuating & wiring also taking an active part in the mixed fighting in the WOOD. The 2 platoons "C" Coy. were not so successful in getting the WOOD. 1½ platoons only getting here before hostile Artillery & M.G. fire became so intense as to prevent them leaving the shelter north of the ravine N.W. of CATERPILLAR. The digging of the C.T. also had to be abandoned & considerable casualties were sustained.	
	10		About 1.0 p.m. 10th inst. orders were received from H.Q. 114 Bde. to endeavour to support the attack on the wood. In compliance with this order the Coy. Lewis Guns were brought into action from the north west of the ravine and ordered to keep the north end of the WOOD under fire. The situation in the WOOD was very obscure at this time & more definite fire orders could not be given for fear of hitting our own men. 1 platoon was invited to endeavour to get into the WOOD from the eastern flank & create a diversion. As soon as company was left the Officer & 6 men were immediately shot down, the platoon was ordered to retire therefore. At 8.0 p.m. seeing it was impossible to get into the WOOD from the east the hostile Artillery having slackened orders were issued for the 3 platoons (less two casualties) to return to bivouac for rest & rations at MINDEN POST. These platoons plus in relief of "A" & "B" Coys. The following is a piece of the Battn "A" Coy. reports. These Coys. being under orders of 113 Inf. Bde. I detached from the Battn "A" Coy. Headquarters 3.0 a.m. DANTZIC ALLEY. At 9.0 a.m. advanced to QUEENS NULLAH. Orders were received to dig a C.T. between CLIFF & SKIP trenches. 2 platoons were employed on this & 2 in assisting to dig trenches by a cross roads in the WOOD. The CLIFF & SKIP trench platoons being taken off this work for the purpose of carrying were etc. At 4.0 p.m. 10th inst. the Coy. received orders to garrison CLIFF trench with 2 platoons, the whole Coy. shortly afterwards occupying this on the 80 yard line, the 2 platoons left in garrison, having	O.A.B.

Instructions regarding War Diaries and Intelligence Summaries are contained in F.S. Regs., Part II. and the Staff Manual respectively. Title Pages will be prepared in manuscript.

INTELLIGENCE SUMMARY

(Erase heading not required.)

19th Welsh.

Place	Date	Hour	Summary of Events and Information	Remarks and references to Appendices
July	10		Men sent up to assist. The line was nearly completed when orders were received to fall back on a 300 yd. line and dig in again. After this there was a further retirement owing to confusion. 2 Platoons remained digging on the 300 yd. line. 2 retired back to their original position as garrison at the X roads. They returned to MINDEN POST lines at 10.45 a.m. 11 inst, having been working carrying & fighting continuously since about 6.0 p.m. night of 9th. They were eventually relieved by details & three platoons of "C" Coy ordered back by me on the night of the 10th inst.	0143
	11th		D. Coy. furnished 1 platoon on French Mortar emplacements QUEENS NULLAH night 9th -10th inst. 2 emplacements, with dug-outs & ammunition pits were completed. At 1.30 a.m. this platoon was reinforced by another to comply with 113 Bde. O.O. as to position of troops at this hour. 2 platoons assembled DANTZIG ALLEY at 5.0 a.m. 10th inst. At 8.0 a.m. 10th inst. an order was received to take these 2 platoons to HALTE for ammunition. On arrival there no ammunition was to be found. The O.C. Coy eventually sent therefore for the Batt's reserve ammunition which was brought up from MINDEN POST. The 2 platoons in QUEENS NULLAH were moved into the wood & consolidated strong points at junction of WOOD Trench & STRIP Trench. Later the whole Bayonne employed on burying. The total casualties of the Batt'n during these operations were, 1 Officer killed, 3 Officers wounded, Other ranks, killed 12, died of wounds - 2, wounded - 106, missing - 15, some of which may be accounted for as stragglers.	0143
	12th	9.30 p.m.	Batt'n less details left in MAMETZ WOOD moved with Batt's Transport to bivouac at CITADEL CAMP, where the details rejoined early on 12th.	0143
	13th		Orders received. Batt'n marched to station at GROVETOWN CAMP to entrain for LONG PRE. - Train due 6.2.0 p.m. left at 6.30. - arrived 5.0 a.m. 13th inst. Batt.	0143

1875. Wt. W593/826 1,000,000 4/15 J.B.C. & A. A.D.S.S./Forms/C. 2118.

INTELLIGENCE SUMMARY 19th Welsh.

(Erase heading not required.)

Instructions regarding War Diaries and Intelligence Summaries are contained in F.S. Regs, Part II. and the Staff Manual respectively. Title Pages will be prepared in manuscript.

Place	Date	Hour	Summary of Events and Information	Remarks and references to Appendices
LONGPRE.	13th		detrained and marched to GORENFLOS. 8 miles.	O.J.J.B
GORENFLOS.	14th		Rested in billets.	O.J.J.B
	15th		Battn. moved by motor bus to THIEVRES.	O.J.J.B
	16th & 17th		At THIEVRES.	O.J.J.B
SAILLY	18th		Left THIEVRES at 9.0 a.m. marched to bivouac at THE DELL J.17.a. Map 57.D	O.J.J.B
AUX BOIS.	19th		Lt. Col. D. GRANT-DALTON left to take comd. of 17th R.W.F. Maj. G.H. EARLE assumed comd. of the unit. in accordance with 38th Divn. instructions - C.O. and Coy. Commanders reconnoitred trenches etc. in 300 yds line.	O.J.J.B
	20th		Work on trench improvement commenced.	O.J.J.B
	21st		" " " continued.	O.J.J.B
	22nd		" " " "	O.J.J.B
	23rd		" " " "	O.J.J.B
	24th		" " " "	O.J.J.B
	25th		" " " " In accordance with instructions received 24th/25th 2 Coys. commenced work on new Rifle front taken over night of 24th - the remaining 2 Coys. "A" + "B" continued work. One to each original Rifle front	O.J.J.B

INTELLIGENCE SUMMARY
(Erase heading not required.)

Instructions regarding War Diaries and Intelligence Summaries are contained in F.S. Regs., Part II. and the Staff Manual respectively. Title Pages will be prepared in manuscript.

Place	Date	Hour	Summary of Events and Information	Remarks and references to Appendices
SAILLY BOIS.	2nd 27		Work on trenches of 300 yd line continued.	02373
	28.	11-30 AM.	Batt. left the Dell at and marched into camp at WARNIMONT WOOD.	02373
	29		Rested in Camp.	
	30	9-15 AM.	Hd Qrs and 3 Coys left WARNIMONT WOOD and marched to camp at AUTHIEULE.	02378
	"	"	"B" Coy " " " " to BEAUVAL. into Billets	
	31.	6-30 AM.	Hd Qrs and 3 Coys left AUTHIEULE marched to railhead at DOULLENS. entrained at 8/30 am. detrained at HOPOUTRE SIDING 3.30 P.M. and marched to billets at HOUTKERQUE. at 7.45 PM.	02378
		6-0 AM.	"B" Coy left BEAUVAL and marched to CANDAS. entrained at 11-30 AM for ST OMER. detrained at 4-15 PM. and proceeded by bus at 9.15 PM to billets at HOUTKERQUE.	02378

J. Hunton Lt. Col.
Comm. 19th Batt. R.

Army Form C. 2118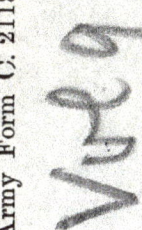

WAR DIARY
or
INTELLIGENCE SUMMARY 19th week.
(Erase heading not required.)

Instructions regarding War Diaries and Intelligence Summaries are contained in F.S. Regs., Part II. and the Staff Manual respectively. Title Pages will be prepared in manuscript.

Place	Date	Hour	Summary of Events and Information	Remarks and references to Appendices
HOUTKERQUE	1-8.16 All Day		Hd Qrs and 3 Coys in billets. "B" Coy. arrived 2-0 A.M.	
F. CAMP. A. 16. C.	2.	11-30 A.M.	Battn. moved to F. CAMP. A. 16. C. BELGIUM. Sheet 28. via St. JANTER-BAIZON. with 2 hours halt for dinners - settled in Camp at 6-0 P.M.	
	3		Parade & inspection by Coy's.	
	4.		"A" and "B" Coys moved to billets in YPRES. 1. 7. D. attached 29th Division Transport Parked at H. 1. D. Sheet 28.	
	5		"C" and "D" Coys moved to dug-out shelters in Canal Bank C. 25. a attached to Dernam Transport parked at G. 4. b. Hd Q.M. Coy. remained at F. Camp.	
	6.		H. Q. Coy. remained at F. Camp. Carried on Camp improvement. Physical Drill & Inspection.	Do - 2nd LT. T. C. Thomas to Hospital. 7. 8. 16.
	7.		Do.	Do - "A" Coy. 3 gassed. " - " 1. shellshock
	8.	11-0 P.M.	Gas alarm called. Hd Qr "Coy - ordered to stand to - Casualties reported.	"B" - 3 gassed.
	9.		H. Q. Coy. remained at F. Camp. Carried on Camp improvement. Physical drill & inspection. Capt Geo Porteous. " to hospital 9.8.16.	Do.
	10.		Do.	Do - one wounded
	11.		Do.	Do - one wounded
	12.		Do.	Do - one wounded

Army Form C. 2118

WAR DIARY
or
INTELLIGENCE SUMMARY 19th Welsh
(Erase heading not required.)

Instructions regarding War Diaries and Intelligence Summaries are contained in F.S. Regs., Part II. and the Staff Manual respectively. Title Pages will be prepared in manuscript.

Place	Date	Hour	Summary of Events and Information	Remarks and references to Appendices
F. CAMP.	13.8.16	All day	H.Q. Coy remained at F. Camp. Carried on Camp improvements. Physical drill and inspection and shell shock.	
	14	do.	do. CAPTN GEO PORTEOUS. Invalided to ENGLAND. (SICK).	
	15	do.	do.	
	16	do.	do. MAJOR R. LLOYD GEORGE } to Hospital.	
	17	do.	do. CAPTN W.A.R. RICHARDS } to Hospital. 2nd LIEUT J.H. JENKINS }	
	18	do.	do.	
	19	do.	do. LIEUT F.C. AUSTIN. } to Hospital. LIEUT A.E. EVANS. }	
	20	do.	do.	
	21		A. and B. Coys moved from YPRES I.7d to killed in TROIS TOURS. B 28. C.O.9. All day. remained at F. Camp. Camp improvements. Physical drill & inspection were carried out. Z + B Coys Transport returned to 'F' Camp. All 4 Coys Coys relieved the 4 Div. Division on the night of 20/21 of August who relieved the 4 Div. Division on the night of 20/21 of August under orders of the 38th Division.	
	22		H.Q. Coy. Carried on Camp improvements. Physical drill and inspection All Coys carried on trench improvement under orders of the G.H.Q. 38th Dis C + D Coys Transport returned to F camp.	

WAR DIARY
or
INTELLIGENCE SUMMARY 19th Welsh

Army Form C. 2118

Place	Date	Hour	Summary of Events and Information	Remarks and references to Appendices
F CAMP.	23.8.16	all day	Camp improvements, Drill and inspection. A.B.C & D Coys Trench Improvements	
	24	do	do	do 1 Major R. Lloyd George returned from hospital
	25	do	do	do (2 wounded)
	26	do	do	do
	27	do	do	do
	28	do	do	do Lieut A.E. Evans invalided to England (Sick)
	29	do	do	do
	30	do	do	do Capt W.A.R. Richards. 2nd Lieut J.H. Jenkins returned from hospital
	31	do	do	

Arundel? Lt Col
Comdg 14th Welsh (Pioneers)

Army Form C. 2118

WAR DIARY
or
INTELLIGENCE SUMMARY 19TH (PIONEER) BATTN WELSH REGT.

(Erase heading not required.)

Vol IV

Place	Date	Hour	Summary of Events and Information	Remarks and references to Appendices
"F" CAMP.	1-9th	All day	H.Q. Coy. Camp improvements. Drill and explosives. A, B, C, & D Coys Trench improvements. Captn M.H. Roffey to hospital. 2 O.R.s wounded.	
	2	"	do.	do. Captn R.H. Davies to hospital.
	3	"	do.	do.
	4		do. moved to WELSH FARM.	do. 2/Lieut Vivian Greatrex Knepp joins unit.
	5		do. Billet improvements and explosives	do.
	6	"	do.	do.
	7		do.	do. 1 O.R. wounded. O.D.B
	8		do.	do.
	9		do.	do.
	10.		do. Transport moved to neighbourhood of HOSPITAL FARM.	do. 1 O.R. killed. Captn Roffey from hospital
	11		do.	do. 2nd Lt Hubert Gordon Bailey 1 O.R. wounded. 2nd Lt Roger Michell Sampson } Join unit.
	12		do.	do.
	13		do.	do.

WAR DIARY
or
INTELLIGENCE SUMMARY 19th (PIONEER) Battn WELSH REGT.

Army Form C. 2118

(Erase heading not required.)

Place	Date	Hour	Summary of Events and Information	Remarks and references to Appendices
WELSH FARM	14.	All day	Hd. Qrs billets improvements - drills, Inspections. A. B. C & D Coys Trench improvements.	
	15	do	do do	
	16	do	do do 2ND LIEUT. ROBERT FRANCIS HUGH DUNCAN joins Unit.	
	17	do	do do	
	18	do	do do	
	19	do	do do	B.D.B.
	20	do	do do LIEUT ROBERT EDWARD WEST joins Unit	
	21	do	do do one O.R. killed one O.R. wounded.	
	22	do	do do	
	23	do	do do 2ND FRANCIS NEVIL WILSON FOX joins Unit	
	24	do	do do C.O. Lieut Col Nugent Dalton on leave to ENGLAND CAPTAIN R.H. DAVIES. from HOSPITAL	

Army Form C. 2118

WAR DIARY
or
INTELLIGENCE SUMMARY

19th (Pioneer) Battn Welsh Regt

(Erase heading not required.)

Place	Date	Hour	Summary of Events and Information	Remarks and references to Appendices
WELSH FARM	25	ALL DAY	H.d Coy buy Bullet improvements - Drills, inspections. A, B, C & D Coys. Trench improvements. MAJOR R. LLOYD GEORGE. Transferred to 135 Army Troops Coy. R.E.	OIII3
	26	"	Do. 2nd Lieut. ARTHUR CYRIL FRETTINGHAM. Do. 2nd " HYWEL LLEWELLYN HUMPHREYS. } Joined Unit	OIII3
	27	"	Do. A, B, C & D Coys. Trench improvements. One O.R. wounded.	
	28	"	Do. Do.	
	29	"	Do. One O.R. wounded. Do.	OIII3
	30	"	Do. Two O.R. wounded. Do.	

R.W. Earle Major
O.C. 19th Welsh

WAR DIARY or INTELLIGENCE SUMMARY

Army Form C. 2118

19 Welsh Regt Vol II

117
3 sheets

Place	Date	Hour	Summary of Events and Information	Remarks and references to Appendices
WELSH FARM	1	10,11,(All day)	Ad Gskay. Billet improvements, inspection, drills. A.B.C.D Coys trench improvements	OpOrd 3
	2	"	Do	OpOrd 3
	3	"	Do	OpOrd 3
	4	"	Do	OpOrd 3
	5	"	Do 2.Lt Vivian Greatrex Knapp to Laundries.	OpOrd 3
	6		do (2 O.R. wounded) do	OpOrd 3
	7		do do	OpOrd 3
	8		do do	OpOrd 3
	9		do C.O. Lieut Col dG grant Dalton returns from leave.	OpOrd 3
	10		do do	OpOrd 3
	11		do (1. O.R. wounded) do	OpOrd 3
	12		do do	OpOrd 3
			do (2 O.R wounded) do	OpOrd 3
			do do	OpOrd 3
			do do	OpOrd 3
			do do	OpOrd 3
			do do Lieut L. Edwards returns from hospital	OpOrd 3

WAR DIARY
or
INTELLIGENCE SUMMARY 19 (Pioneer) Batt^n Welsh Regt.

Army Form C. 2118

(Erase heading not required.)

Place	Date	Hour	Summary of Events and Information	Remarks and references to Appendices
Welsh Farm.	13.10.16	All Day	Hd Qrs Roy Billet, improvements, inspections, drills. A.B.C & D Coys trench improvements	O.4.13.
	14.	"	do	O.4.13.
	15.	"	do Lt. S. Thomas To Hospital	O.5.13.
	16.	"	do O.R. 2 Killed 1 Wounded	O.4.13.
	17.	"	do do	O.4.13.
	18.	"	do Capt W.E. Davies from Hospital	O.4.13.
	19.	"	do do	O.4.13.
	20.	"	do Lt G.N. Tregarthen to Hospital	O.4.13.
	21.	"	do O.R. 1 Wounded. do	O.4.13.
	22.	"	do do	O.4.13.
	23.	"	do Capt J.P. Emett to Hospital do	O.4.13.

WAR DIARY
or
INTELLIGENCE SUMMARY 19 (PIONEER) BATTN WELSH REGT.

Army Form C. 2118

(Erase heading not required.)

Place	Date	Hour	Summary of Events and Information	Remarks and references to Appendices
WELSH FARM	24.10.16	ALL DAY.	HQ Coy. Billet improvements. A.B.C & D Coys Trench improvements.	
	25.		do. Inspections drills. Lt L S. THOMAS. to ENGLAND (SICK).	Appx.
	26.		do. do.	Appx.
	27.		do. do.	Appx.
	28.		do. do.	Appx.
	29.		do. do. 2ND LIEUT. REGINALD JOHN ELDRED. Joins Unit	Appx.
	30.		do. do.	Appx.
	31.		do. do.	Appx.

Thow Tallor Lt Col
Comdg 19th Welsh Regt

Army Form C. 2118

WAR DIARY
or
INTELLIGENCE SUMMARY

(Erase heading not required.)

19TH PIONEER BATTN WELSH REGT.

Vol 12

127
3 sheets

Place	Date	Hour	Summary of Events and Information	Remarks and references to Appendices
YPRES Salient	Nov 1916			
	1.		H.Q. at Walk Farm. A+B. Coys at TRois Tours. C+D. Canal Bank – Work on C.T's + drainage	0279.
	2.		Batt'n rest day. Bathing - Inspections	0279.
	3.		Work on C.T's and drainage continued – All Coys HTR carry on Billet Improvement	0279.
	4.		Do do	0278
	5.		Do do	
	6.		Do do	
	7.		Do do	one O.R. wounded
	8.		Do do New EALING TRENCH by B. Coy. and from the NILE needed front line	0079
	9.		Do do	
	10.		Do do 2 – 5.9 shells fell my close to HTR billet.	
	11.		Batt'n Rest Day – Bathing + Inspections –	
	12.		H.Q. Coy. Billet improvements inspections, drill. A.B.C.D. Coys Trench improvements	0079
	13.		Do Do	
	14.		Do Do	
	15.		Do Do	

WAR DIARY
or
INTELLIGENCE SUMMARY

Army Form C. 2118

19TH PIONEER BATTN. WELSH REGT.

(Erase heading not required.)

Place	Date	Hour	Summary of Events and Information	Remarks and references to Appendices
YPRES SALIENT	Nov 1916 16.		H.Q. at WELSH FARM. A & B Coys at TROIS TOURS. C & D Coys Canal Bank Trench improvements	O.O.43.
	17.		Coy inspections. Drills, kitted improvements. A.B.C & D Coys. Trench improvements.	
	18.		do.	
	19.		do.	
	20.		do.	
	21.		WELSH FARM set on fire by enemy's shells. H.Q. Coy employed in salving kits and equipments etc. Extinguishing fire. O.R. 1 killed 1 wounded.	O.O.R.
	22.		H.Q. Coy distributed between Coys at TROIS TOURS. CANAL BANK and TRANSPORT LINES	O.O.B.
	23.		H.Q. C & D. Canal Bank. A & B. at TROIS TOURS. Trench improvements. MAJOR G.H. EARLE to hospital	O.O.B.
	24.		do Trench improvements	
	25.		do	
	26.		do	
	27.		do	

WAR DIARY
or
INTELLIGENCE SUMMARY

19th PIONEER BATTn. WELSH REGT.

(Erase heading not required.)

Army Form C. 2118

Place	Date	Hour	Summary of Events and Information	Remarks and references to Appendices
YPRES SALIENT	Nov 28	1916.	H.Q. C & A Coys. CANAL BANK. A.B. Coys - TROIS TOURS. Trench improvements	Apx 8
	29		do do do	
	30		do do do	

Hawkins? Lt Col
Comdg 19th Welsh Regt

Army Form C. 2118

WAR DIARY
or
INTELLIGENCE SUMMARY
(Erase heading not required.)

19th Batt: The Welsh Regt. (Pioneers)

Place	Date 1916	Hour	Summary of Events and Information	Remarks and references to Appendices
YPRES - SALIENT.	Dec 1st		HQ and 2 Coys in Canal Bank - 2 Coys at Truro Towers - Transport Hospital Farm.	
J. Camp.	2nd		Handed over billets and work to 13th Gloucester Pioneers. HQ and 4 Coys. marched to J. Camp. Transport marched to WORMHOUDT.	
	3rd		Inspection by the G.O.C.	
HOULLE	4th		HQ and 4 Coys. marched to POPERINGHE and entrained for ST. OMER. Transport marched to billets at MOULLE. HQ and 4 Coys. detrained at ST. OMER and marched to billets. 1. Coy. at MOULLE remained in adjoining village of HOULLE.	
	5th		Batt. rested in billets. C.O. and 2nd C. inspected site of proposed Rifle Range.	
	6th		Work commenced on Range. Training of details in Signalling and Lewis gun commenced.	
	7th		Work on Range and training of details continued.	
	8th		do do	
	9th		do do	
	10th		do do	

WAR DIARY
or
INTELLIGENCE SUMMARY 19th (Pioneer) Batt" The Welsh Regt.

Army Form C. 2118

Place	Date	Hour	Summary of Events and Information	Remarks and references to Appendices
HOULLE	11th Dec.		Work on Range and training of Signallers and Lewis Gunners continues.	Appendix to Diary
	12th	"	do	
	13th	"	do	
	14th	"	do	
	15th	"	do	
	16th	"	do	
	17th	"	do	
	18th	"	do	
	19th	"	do 2nd Lt. G.C. LEWIS proceeded to join B Batt" H.M.G.C.	
	20th	"	do	
	21st	"	do Capt R.H. DAVIES proceeded to report to D.L.R.R. (temporarily att'd)	
	22nd	"	do Range inspected by Army Commander	
	23rd	"	B. Range completed.	
	24th	"	Work commenced on A. Range	

Army Form C. 2118

WAR DIARY
or
INTELLIGENCE SUMMARY 19th (Pioneer) Batt" The Welsh Regt
(Erase heading not required.)

Place	Date	Hour	Summary of Events and Information	Remarks and references to Appendices
HULLE	25 Dec		Xmas Day. No work done. Concert with 151 Coy R.E.	Original Entry
	26"		Work on A Range resumed & Training of Signallers and Lewis Gunners.	
	27 "		Do do	
	28 "		Do do	
	29 "		Do do	
	30 "		Do do 2nd Lieut F.N.W. FOX proceeded to join 14th Welsh.	
	31 "		Do do	

Rhun Walsh Lieut Col.
Comdg 19th (Pioneer) Batt"
The Welsh Regt

Army Form C. 2118

WAR DIARY
or
INTELLIGENCE SUMMARY
19th (Pioneer) Batt. The Welsh Regt.
(Erase heading not required.)

Place	Date	Hour	Summary of Events and Information	Remarks and references to Appendices
HOULLE	1st Jan. 1917		Work on A. Range - for Musketry Training School of 2nd Army.	
	2	"	Work on Range continued, and Training of Signallers and Lewis Gun teams continued. Training of Signallers and Lewis Gun teams continued.	
	3	"	Do.	
	4	"	'A' & 'D' Coys work on Range. 'B' Coy. march to billets at TOURNETTE.	2nd Lieut. ALBERT BERTIE VAUGHAN Joins Unit.
	5	"	'A' & 'D' Coys complete work on A Range. 'C' Coy march to billets at LENLINE.	Do.
			'C' & 'B' " commence work on Range Q 35	
QUELMES	6	"	H.Q. Coy. march to billets at QUELMES. 'A' Coy march to billets at ZUDAUSQUES.	
			'D' " " " AUDENTHUN.	2nd Lieut. STANLEY DAVIES rejoining from sick leave.
	7	"	A. B. C. & D. Coys work on Range.	H.Q. Coy. Training. Drills Inspections.
	8	"	Do.	Do.
				C.O. proceeds on leave.
	9	"	Do.	Do.
				2nd Lieut. R.J. ELDRED rejoins from sick leave.

Army Form C. 2118

WAR DIARY
or
INTELLIGENCE SUMMARY
(Erase heading not required.)

19th (Pioneers) Welsh Regt.

Place	Date	Hour	Summary of Events and Information	Remarks and references to Appendices
QUELMES.	10. Jan. 1917.		A.B.C. & D. Coys. work on Range. H.Q. Coy. Training Drills, Inspections. 2nd Lieut. HERBERT CECIL MILLER } 2nd " TOM LEONARD JONES. } Joins Unit 2nd " GEORGE EDMUND PRITCHARD }	Re Blank
"	11.		"A" "B" "C" & "D" Coys. work on Range. H.Q. Coy. continue Training etc. 2nd Lieut. JOHN BRADFORD. reports for duty with M.C.C. (A. Branch).	
"	12.		"A" & B. Coys. March off at 5.45 a.m. from COURMETTE and entrain at ST. MOMELIN at 9/30 a.m. for TROIS TOURS. 2nd Lieut. R.J. ELDRED to hospital.	
"	13.		Transport move by road to HOSPITAL FARM. "C" and "D" Coy. finish work on Range. A "B" 6 a.m. commence French work. A "B" 6 a.m. entrain at St. MOMELIN 9.40 a.m.	
YPRES. SALIENT.	14.		H.Qs "C" & "D" Coys march from KILLS 5 a.m. for CANAL BANK.	
"	15.		H.Q Coy. Drills. Inspections etc. A.B.C. & D. Coys. French Improvements. 2nd Lieut. ERNEST JAMES MATHIAS. } Joins 2nd " JOHN DAVID WALTERS. } Unit Lieut. F.C. AUSTIN. to hospital.	
"	16.		Do. Do.	

Army Form C. 2118

WAR DIARY
or
INTELLIGENCE SUMMARY 19th (PIONEERS) WELSH REGT.
(Erase heading not required.)

Instructions regarding War Diaries and Intelligence Summaries are contained in F. S. Regs., Part II. and the Staff Manual respectively. Title Pages will be prepared in manuscript.

Place	Date	Hour	Summary of Events and Information	Remarks and references to Appendices
YPRES SALIENT.	17 Jan.		21 Q. Coy. Inspection, Drills, Billet Inspt. A.B.C. & D Coys. Trench Improvements.	
	18.	"	do. do.	
	19.	"	do. Draft of 64 O.R. arrive at Camp "A" Reinforcements	
	20.	"	do. do.	
	21.	"	do. do.	
	22.	"	do. do.	
	23.	"	do. do.	
	24.	"	do. do.	C.O. returns from leave.
	25.	"	do. do.	1 O.R. killed (bullet)
	26.	"	do. do.	
	27.	"	do. do.	
	28.	"	4 O.R. killed in billets at TROIS TOURS. (SHELLS) do.	
	29.	"	do. do. B Coy. move to PELLISIER FARM.	
	30.	"	do. do.	
	31.	"	do. do.	

Army Form C. 2118

WAR DIARY
or
INTELLIGENCE SUMMARY 19th (PIONEER) 13th WELSH REGT.
(Erase heading not required.)

Place	Date	Hour	Summary of Events and Information	Remarks and references to Appendices
YPRES-SALIENT	Feb. 1917. 1st		H.Q. & C. and D. Coys in dug outs Canal Bank W. A. and B. Coys in Farm PALLISIER A. Coy at Chateau des TROIS TOURS. Transport Lines at Hospital Farm.	
			All Coys. employed on work in trenches and small parties building new dugouts accommodation at all billets.	
	2nd & 3rd		Do. do. do.	
	4th		Do. do. do. casualties 1 O.R. killed	
	5th & 6th		Do. do. do.	
	7th		Do. do. do. 3. O.R. wounded	
	8th		Do. do. do. (1. O.R. died of wounds.)	
	9th		Do. do. do. 1. O.R. killed	
	10th		Do. do. do. 5. O.R. wounded	
	11th & 12th		Do. do. do.	
	13th		Do. do. do. 2. O.R. wounded. 2nd Lieut. H.L. DAVIES joined for duty. Lieut. R.S. PALMER rejoined.	

Army Form C. 2118

WAR DIARY
or
INTELLIGENCE SUMMARY   19th (PIONEER) 13th WELSH REGT
(Erase heading not required.)

Place	Date	Hour	Summary of Events and Information	Remarks and references to Appendices
YPRES SALIENT.	Feb. 1917. 14th		All Coys employed on work in trenches & parties on billet improvements	
	15th		B.Coy preparing move & dugout in Canal Bank preparatory to moving there from PALLISIER FARM.	
			Do. do. do. Casualties 2nd Lieut. C.F. TAYLOR wounded. 1. O.R. wounded.	POTS.
	16th,17th,18th		Do. do. do. 2nd Lieut. C.F. TAYLOR died of wounds 18th buried in Military Cemetery near PROVEN. Map 27. F.7.a.8.2. Row F. plot 2. No.14.	OOTB.
	19th		Do. do. do. B.Coy take over billets in Canal Bank.	
	20th		Do. do. do. Casualties 1. O.R. killed.	
	21st, 22nd, 23rd, 24th		Do. do. do. An appreciation of work on Ranges rec'd from C.E. 2nd Army - att'd copy	
	25th		Do. do. do. 5. O.R. killed - 16 wounded.	OOTB

Army Form C. 2118

WAR DIARY
or
INTELLIGENCE SUMMARY 19th (PIONEER) BATTn WELSH REGt
(Erase heading not required.)

Place	Date	Hour	Summary of Events and Information	Remarks and references to Appendices
YPRES SALIENT	Feb. 1917 25th	Cont'd	These casualties were caused by hostile shell fire during our enemy movement on trenches near which working parties of two Coys this Battn were employed. A Coy & D. Coy parties were caught in the barrage. 2nd Lieut W.H. Phillips displayed great courage and devotion to duty and also No 31932 Corpl F. Lewis of B. Coy who was recommended for & awarded a Divl. Distinguished Conduct Certificate by the Maj. Gen. Comdg 38th Divn	OX73.
	26th		All Coys employed on work in trenches and field improvements in Canal Bank.	OX73.
	27th		Do Do	
	28th		Do Do	
	Feb. 18th 1917		Capt R.B. Maddocks (Journey) to ST POL there invested with the CROIX DE GUERRE avec PALME by Genl NIVELLE. Cen C. French Armies in France.	OX73.

Shannolain JR
Comd 19th Welsh Regt

Army Form C. 2118

WAR DIARY
or
INTELLIGENCE SUMMARY
(Erase heading not required.)

Place	Date	Hour	Summary of Events and Information	Remarks and references to Appendices
			Precis of 2nd Army E.4698. add'd to VIII Corps dated 20.2.17. I have to draw your attention to the excellent work that has been done by the Rifle Ranges in the neighbourhood of TILQUES by Sapper units in your Corps, especially — — and the 19th West Riding Pioneer Batt — — — I am especially pleased by the work of the two Pioneer Battalions which exceeded my expectations both as to quantity and quality. — (Sd) J.M. GRUBB Major General Chief Engineer Second Army	

Army Form C. 2118

WAR DIARY
or
INTELLIGENCE SUMMARY 19th (PIONEER) Bn WELSH REGT

Vol 16

167
2 sheets

Place	Date	Hour	Summary of Events and Information	Remarks and references to Appendices
YPRES SALIENT	March 1917. 1st		HdQrs. B.C. and D. Coys in dugouts Canal Bank. W.A. Coy. in billets at Ferme Chateau de Trois Tours. Transport lines at Hospital Farm. All Coys. working on trench improvements. B Coy draining dirt track in addition. Small parties from each Coy. employed on extension and improvement of billets and dugout accommodation.	O.B.
	2nd		Do. do.	
	3rd		Do. do.	
	4th 5th		Do. do.	
	6th 7th		Do. do.	
	8th		Do. do. A. Coy. take over billets at Canal Bank.	
	9th		Do. do. 17. O.R. join Batt. from Reinforcement Camp.	
	10th		Do. do. 2nd Lt. R.J. ELDRED to England sick. 43 O.R. join Batt. from Reinforcement Camp.	
	11th		Do. do. 2nd Lt. D.G. DAVIES joins Batt from 9th Welsh Regt. 2nd Lt. E.J. MATHIAS to England sick	
	12th		Do. do.	
	13th		Do. do. 1 O.R. died of wounds.	

Army Form C. 2118

WAR DIARY
or
INTELLIGENCE SUMMARY
(Erase heading not required.)

Place	Date	Hour	Summary of Events and Information	Remarks and references to Appendices
YPRES SALIENT	14th		All Coys employed on work in Trenches and parties on billet improvements	
	15th		do. do. do. 28 O.R. joined Batt. from reinforcement Camp.	
	16th & 17th		do do do	
	18th & 19th		do do do	
	20th & 21st		do do do	
	22nd		do do do	
	23rd & 24th		do do do Batt. stood to. 4.20 a.m.	
	25th		do do do	
	26th		do do do 1. O.R. killed	
	27th		do do do Transport lines heavily shelled. all animals were removed in safety and temporary lines established Map 28. B. 26. a. 2. b.	
	28th		do do do	
	29th		do do do	
	30th		do do do Transport move to new lines. Map 28. A. 28. B.1.1.	
	31st		do do do	

Frank Walters /TR
Comm'g 19th Welsh Regt.

Army Form C. 2118

19 Welch Rgt
Vol 17

WAR DIARY
or
INTELLIGENCE SUMMARY
(Erase heading not required.)

Instructions regarding War Diaries and Intelligence Summaries are contained in F.S. Regs., Part II. and the Staff Manual respectively. Title Pages will be prepared in manuscript.

Place	Date	Hour	Summary of Events and Information	Remarks and references to Appendices
YPRES SALIENT.	April 1917 1st		All Coy's employed on work in trenches, and parties on billet improvements	
	2nd	do	do	
	3rd & 4th	do	2nd Lt. R.A. GRAY joins from 9th Gordon Highlanders	
	5th	do	do	
	6th	do	do	RFDD
	7th	do	CAPT. W.E. DAVIES struck off strength. One O.R. Wounded	
	8th	do	Test Gas alarm took place	
	9th	do	C.O. attends course at 2nd Army H.Q.	
	10th	do	'A' Coy move to Toronto Fm. and 'B' Coy to Rowsell Fm.	
	11th & 12th	do	1 O.R. killed. 2 O.R. Wounded.	
	13th	do	C.O. returns from course.	
	14th	do	Test Gas Alarm took place	
	15th	do	1 O.R Wounded.	
	16th	do	17 O.R. join Battalion from Reinforcement Camp.	
	17th	do	C.O. goes on leave.	
	18th	do	do	
	19th & 20	do	Gloucester Pioneers take over work	E.O 17.7 2 sheet
	21st & 22	do	do	

WAR DIARY
or
INTELLIGENCE SUMMARY

(Erase heading not required.)

Army Form C. 2118

Place	Date	Hour	Summary of Events and Information	Remarks and references to Appendices
YPRES SALIENT	23rd		All days employed on work in the trenches, and parties on killer improvement	R.7.D.D.
	24th		do. do. Batt. stood to at 11/pm. 2 O.R. wounded	
	25th + 26th		do do 1 O.R. Wounded.	
	27th + 28th		do do	
	29th		do 2nd Lts. B.J. ISAAC, D.B. SAMWAYS and H.M. WILLIAMS joined Batt. Major G.H. EARLE struck off strength with effect from 24th March 1917. War Office letter 93806/16 (M.S.K) and C in C Letter 29.4.17.	
	30th		do do C.O. returns off leave.	

Commdg. 19th Welch Regt.

Army Form C. 2118

WAR DIARY
or
INTELLIGENCE SUMMARY 19th (Pioneer) Batt. Welsh Regt.

(Erase heading not required.)

Place	Date	Hour	Summary of Events and Information	Remarks and references to Appendices
YPRES SALIENT	1st May. 1917.		Location H.Q. and 3 Coys. Canal Bank (B.Coy. moved from Roussel Farm today to Mouton Farm) and A.Coy. to Canal Bank. Transport at A.9.a.2.3. Sheet 28.NW. 1/20,000.	
	2nd		All Coys. working in trenches and parties on billet improvements etc.	
	3rd		Work continues. Gas Alarm. Stand To 11pm. no gas noticeable.	
			Do. do. Bell. Stew to 11.30 pm on Gas Alarm something — fumes — to false alarm.	
	4th		Work continues.	
	5th		Do. do.	
	6th		Do. do. B.Coy billets shelled heavily Coy moved out to paddk. 1. O.R. wounded.	
	7th		" " "	
	8th		" " " 1. enemy shell near Canal Bank 3. O.R. killed 5. wounded	
	9th		" " "	
	10th		" " "	
	11th		" " "	
	12th		" B.Coy move to canvas camp Steentje Mill A.17.a.	

Army Form C. 2118

WAR DIARY
or
INTELLIGENCE SUMMARY 19th (Pioneer) Battn Welsh Regt
(Erase heading not required.)

Instructions regarding War Diaries and Intelligence Summaries are contained in F.S. Regs., Part II. and the Staff Manual respectively. Title Pages will be prepared in manuscript.

Place	Date	Hour	Summary of Events and Information	Remarks and references to Appendices
YPRES SALIENT	May 13th	1917.	All Coys. working in trenches and quarries on dug-outs in Canal Bank Area. Constructing new dug-outs E. bank Canal D. increasing cover W. bank.	
	14th		Do. do.	
	15th & 16th		Do. do. 1. O.R. killed 1. wounded.	
	17th & 18th		Do. do.	
	19th & 20		Do. do.	
	21 & 22		Do. do.	
	23rd		Do. do. R.S.M. Reynolds joined Bn. to replace R.S.M. Lloyd.	
	24 & 25		Do. do. R.S.M. Lloyd proceded to Base en route to England on relief.	
	26 & 27		Do. do.	
	28th		Do. do. Gas alarm 2.30 a.m. all ranks Stood To. Stood To ordered by 114th Inf. Bde H.qrs.	
	29 & 30		Do. do. 1. O.R. wounded morning of 30th	
	31st		Do. do.	

J Huntleton Lt.Col.
Cmdg 19th Welsh Regt.

Army Form C. 2118

WAR DIARY
or
INTELLIGENCE SUMMARY 19TH (PIONEER) BN WELSH REGT
(Erase heading not required.)

Vol 19

Place	Date	Hour	Summary of Events and Information	Remarks and references to Appendices
YPRES SALIENT	1st June 1917		Location - H.Q. and 3 Coys in Canvas Camp near STEENTJE FARM A.17d. Transport A.9a.2.3 SHEET 28.N.W. All Coys working in trenches and parties constructing new dugouts in east Canal Bank near Bridge 6. and improving existing dugouts at own billets - Work continued	
	2nd-3rd		Do. do.	
	4th		Do. do. Hostile gas shell bombardment of YPRES and battery positions - Gas (chiefly lachrymatory) strong in Canal Bank - from 11 pm till 3 am 5th May - Stood to will New Respirators on - 4 OR evacuates suffering from effects of gas.	
	5th		do. do. Capt. L.S. THOMAS rejoined - Noted in Times Birthday from London Gazette - Lt Col D.Grant Dalton awarded D.S.O. - Casualties - 2nd Lt H.L. HUMPHREYS and 2 OR wounded (shells).	
	6th		do. do.	

Army Form C. 2118.

WAR DIARY
or
INTELLIGENCE SUMMARY. 19TH (PIONEER) BN WELSH REGT
(Erase heading not required.)

Place	Date	Hour	Summary of Events and Information	Remarks and references to Appendices
YPRES SALIENT	7th		Work continued. Heavy shells near T. Lines. 1 O.R. Horse killed	
	8th	9/15	Do. do. Lines moved to A.14.b.	
	10th		Do. do.	
	11th		Do. do. 1. O.R. wounded.	
			Do. do. Gas shell alarm. Stood to with Box respirators motored to 1.30am 17th only slight.	
	12th		Do. do. Transport moved to lines at A.28.d.	
	13th		Do. do. Casualties 1. O.R. wounded and 1. killed	
	14th	1	Do. do.	
	15th		Do. do. HQ moved to East Canal Bank at C.19.c.central.	
			At 11.40 p.m. dugouts oscillated and skilaret noise as of exploded mine was noticed.	
	16th		Do. do. HQ moved to dugouts near Bridge 6.	
	17th		Do. do. B.C. and D. Coys arrange new billets	
	18th		Do. do. ditto.	
	19th		Do. do. New billets occupied. Casualties 3 O.R. killed. 7 wounded.	

WAR DIARY
INTELLIGENCE SUMMARY.
(Erase heading not required.)

Army Form C. 2118.

Place	Date	Hour	Summary of Events and Information	Remarks and references to Appendices
YPRES SALIENT	20th		Work Continued	
	21st		Do Casualties 2 O.R's Wounded.	
	22nd		Do do 3 O.R's Wounded.	
	23rd		Do do 2 O.R's Wounded.	
	24th		Do do 4 O.R's Wounded. Capt. A.F. Evans and 2.Lt. H.M. Williams killed. Lt. R.S. Palmer and Lt. J.H. Jenkins Wounded in dug-out on CANAL BANK.	
	25th		Do do 3143b. Act. Corpl. G.W. South "B" Coy awarded Military Medal	
	26th		Do do H.Q. shelled heavily for 2 hrs with 4.2.S. Casualties 2 O.R's Wounded.	
	27th		Do do Casualties. 2 O.R's killed. 1 O.R Wounded. Batt.n moves to Transport lines en route for PROVEN, after 6 months on the CANAL BANK.	

Army Form C. 2118.

WAR DIARY
or
INTELLIGENCE SUMMARY.
(Erase heading not required.)

Instructions regarding War Diaries and Intelligence Summaries are contained in F. S. Regs., Part II. and the Staff Manual respectively. Title pages will be prepared in manuscript.

Place	Date	Hour	Summary of Events and Information	Remarks and references to Appendices
YPRES. SALIENT	28th		Battalion arrived at CENTRAL CAMP, PROVEN. Sgt. D. ORGAN awarded Military Medal. 28/29th Draft of 61 from Reinforcement Camp joins the Battn.	
	29th		Inspection and Drill parades under OC Coys in the morning. Recreational Training in the afternoon. 29/30th Draft of 45 from Reinforcement Camp joins the Battn.	
	30th		Work as for 29th	

J. Sinclair LtCol
Comdg 19th Welsh Regt

Army Form C. 2118.

WAR DIARY
or
INTELLIGENCE SUMMARY. 19th (PIONEER) Batt. WELSH REGT.
(Erase heading not required.)

Vol 20

Place	Date	Hour	Summary of Events and Information	Remarks and references to Appendices
PROVEN	1st July 1917		Drill parades under Coy arrangements - Lewis Gun training and Recreational Training -	Apps 3
	2nd 3rd 4th	Do Do Do	A Coy moved to BOLLEZEELE on 2nd to erect Huts for Convalescent Camp	
	5th	Do Do Do	Draft of 77 O.R. joined Batt.	
	6th 7th 8th	Do Do Do Do		
	9th	Do Do Do	Batt. Sports were held.	DRB
	10th	Do Do Do	Draft of 20 O.R. joined Batt. C Coy on fatigue for R.A.	
	11th	Do Do Do	B Coy moved to Camp at 27/E.11.a.6.5. in training for light railway construction. 1 Off. + 40 O.R. att 55 Coy RE	
	12th 13th		for thirty-rail making. Party of 3 Off. + 100 O.R. furnished for R.A. 14th Corps.	
	14th 15th and 16th	Do Do		
	17th 18th		C and D Coys making tudging mats.	DRB
	19th		A Coy rejoined from BOLLEZEELE. H.Q. and 3 Coys moved to CANAL BANK in relief of 1/2nd Monmouths - by train PROVEN to ELVERDINGHE thence marching by Track 10. Relief complete 4 am 20th Transport moved by road to Camp G. B Coy moved Camp to A.14.a.5.8.	20 7 Feb 3.

Army Form C. 2118.

WAR DIARY
or
INTELLIGENCE SUMMARY. 19th (PIONEER) BATTn WELSH REGT
(Erase heading not required.)

Instructions regarding War Diaries and Intelligence Summaries are contained in F. S. Regs., Part II. and the Staff Manual respectively. Title pages will be prepared in manuscript.

Place	Date	Hour	Summary of Events and Information	Remarks and references to Appendices
YPRES SALIENT	20th July 1917		The 3 Coys. A.C and D. took over repairs and maintenance of C.T.s. and provided cable burying party on nights of 20th and 21st. 1.OR wounded 20th 3. OR wounded and 1 killed 21st	
	22nd		Repair and maintenance of C.T.s. 5 OR wounded. 1.Offr. and 40 OR. moved to ELVERDINGHE CHATEAU for work under orders of C.R.E. 1.OR. wounded	
	23rd		do. do.	
	24 & 25th		do. 1. OR. wounded.	
	26th		do. 4. OR. wounded.	
	27th		do.	
	28th		Det. workd on repair and enlargement of MARENGO CAUSEWAY. By R.E. dugout an MARENGO CAUSEWAY. 2. OR. killed (one only reported) 2. OR. wounded (one only reported) 1. Coyl and 3 men missing. The foregoing include 1 Coyl and 3 men comprising B. Coy. Guard at RIVOLI FARM. The relieving Guard at 6 p.m. found dugout destroyed only one body (oblitrated) and other remains. Remains buried at. 28/. B.24 c.95.85 are supposed	

A6945 Wt.W1142/M1160 35,000 12/16 B.D.&L. Forms/C/2118/14

Army Form C. 2118.

WAR DIARY
INTELLIGENCE SUMMARY. 19TH (PIONEER) BATTN WELSH REGT

(Erase heading not required.)

Instructions regarding War Diaries and Intelligence Summaries are contained in F. S. Regs., Part II. and the Staff Manual respectively. Title pages will be prepared in manuscript.

Place	Date	Hour	Summary of Events and Information	Remarks and references to Appendices
YPRES SALIENT	July 1917			
			to those of 25551 Corpl D. Richards and 31012 Pte E.G. Jones and 54510 Pte D. James were buried on	
			Cemetery at BARD COTTAGE.	A.D.S.
			During the period 20.7.17 to 29.7.17 the effect of enemy gas shells were felt almost nightly in the neighbourhood of B″ Billets CANAL BANK C.19.C.- no cases of serious gassing were caused but a number (42) were inoculated	
			pick (?gasses) between nose and lips.	
X. DAY.	29th		Repairs and maintenance of C.Ts. Carrying Track steels for Artillery Track.	A.O.T.S.
			100 men assisted 1st Coy R.E on MARENGO CAUSEWAY.	
Y. DAY.	30th		do do Transfers allotted as follows A.Coy. SKIPTON and NILE	
			C.Coy. HUDDERSFIELD to FT LINE and COLNE VALLEY.	
			D.Coy. CORRIDOR. HQ & A&D Coy moved to East Bank C.13.S.1.3.	A.O.T.S.
Z. DAY.	31st	ZERO HOUR 3.50 am	Artillery barrage opened promptly. SA/parades and Drills	
			Orders A and D Coy on receipt of report that 'Black Line' had been captured - moved from Billets at 7.30 am and marched 8/hrs	
			forming Artillery Track from HUDDLESTON CROSS ROADS to near	A.O.T.Y.

WAR DIARY
or
INTELLIGENCE SUMMARY.

Army Form C. 2118.

Place	Date	Hour	Summary of Events and Information	Remarks and references to Appendices
YPRES SALIENT	July 3 1917		BOCHE HOUSE returned to Canal Bank 3.30 p.m. Casualties 6. O.R. wounded 0275	
			C. Coy in reserve. Carried beech slabs for road.	

J. Walter Lt Colonel
comdg 19th (Pioneer) Batt
Welsh Regt

Army Form C. 2118.

WAR DIARY
or
INTELLIGENCE SUMMARY. 19TH (PIONEER) BATTN WELSH REGT
(Erase heading not required.)

Place	Date	Hour	Summary of Events and Information	Remarks and references to Appendices
YPRES SALIENT	July 31st		BOCHE HOUSE (returned) to CANAL BANK. 3.30 p.m. Casualties 6 O.R. wounded. C. Coy. in reserve carrying duck slabs for road.	
	Aug 1st		A and D Coys continued track from BOCHE HOUSE to C.8.85.9. Leaving CANAL BANK 5 a.m. returning 6 hrs in continuous rain. C. Coy relieving 123rd Field Coy R.E. on strong point 11 to 17 near IRON CROSS. Leaving killed at 5 a.m. returning 5 p.m. Little progress was made owing to adverse weather — hostile shelling and congestion of troops. A & D Coys also carried duck and transported some 36 lengths of tram line from BELMONT to HARKNESS AVENUE.	
	2nd		C. Coy. burying cables flushing for extension of GLIMPSE COT tramway. D. Coy. in 2 shifts 5 a.m. to 8 p.m. A. Coy & Regt Transport 7 G.S. wagons from but slab track BAIRD CAUSEWAY to HUDDLESTON CROSS ROADS. 5 O.R. wounded.	
	3rd		A and D Coys worked in two shifts 5 a.m. to 8 p.m. on duckboard track continuing WINDSOR CASTLE line to CHEMIN ESTAMINET road S. & K. of PILCKEM MILL. C. Coys. assisting R.E. field Coy on GLIMPSE COT tramway. 5 wagons loading material from ONDANCK.	

Army Form C. 2118.

WAR DIARY
or
INTELLIGENCE SUMMARY. 19TH (PIONEER) BATTN WELSH REGT
(Erase heading not required.)

Place	Date	Hour	Summary of Events and Information	Remarks and references to Appendices
YPRES. A.18.a	1917. Aug. 4th and 5th	Do Do	Do Do	
	6th		H.Q. and A. C. and D. Coys moved to bivouac at A.18.a central near CARDOEN FARM. Work was continued on track slab road. Two Coys daily one Coy in Camp. Coys proceeded by lorries from ONDANCK and returns to same. There were carried on under MAJOR J.C.I. WOOD. 123rd Field Coy R.E.	Ophthalmic Captain Roberts
	7th		Do Do Coy in camp baths. Two Coys kit inspection. Casualties 1 OR wounded	
	8th		Do Do Do Do Camp lightly shelled about 8 pm. " 6 OR wounded	
	9th		Do Do Do Do	
	10th 11th		Do Do Do Do	
	12th		Do Do Relieved after working hours by 13th Welch 1st and 3 Coys moved and Transport moved to PIDDINGTON CAMP in PROVEN area.	
	13th		Parades by Coys and inspection by Company Officers.	
	14th		Do Do Do arm drill and inspections. Working parties from two Coys required been cleans camp ground and curried on clearing chavin Quarters 10 R.B. Coy accounted	

Army Form C. 2118.

WAR DIARY
or
INTELLIGENCE SUMMARY. 19th (PIONEER) BATTy WELSH REGt
(Erase heading not required.)

Instructions regarding War Diaries and Intelligence Summaries are contained in F. S. Regs., Part II. and the Staff Manual respectively. Title pages will be prepared in manuscript.

Place	Date	Hour	Summary of Events and Information	Remarks and references to Appendices
PROVEN AREA	AUGUST 1917			
	15th/16th		Parades by Coys. Drill etc Parties on Camp improvement	
	17th		Do do do HQ 3 Coys moved to Bivouac at A.18.a central by train from PROVEN at 5pm to ELVERDINGHE Huer by march route. Transport returned to G Camp.	
				Casualties 1 OR B/Sgt wounded
	18th		HQ and 3 Coys relieved 11th D.L.I. in Canal Bank C.19.C.0.3 moving by train across country arriving 5.30am. A and C Coys furnished night parties working on improvement trenches etc on GREEN LINE	781 R. O. Map Sheet 20.S.W.4.
				Casualties 4 OR wounded
	19th		Work continued by A and C Coys. D Coy took over work on duck slab road PILCKEM Rd to IRON CROSS, working 2 shifts by day. Regtl Transport was employed hauling wire pickets etc for work on GREEN LINE	
	20th		Do do do Transport moved to A11c.7.6. HOUSSLOW	
	22nd		Do do do Above work taken over by Corps.	

A.6945. Wt. W.14422/M.1160 35,000 12/16 D. D. & L. Forms/C/2118/14.

WAR DIARY

INTELLIGENCE SUMMARY. 19TH (PIONEER) BATTN WELSH REGT.

(Erase heading not required.)

Army Form C. 2118.

Place	Date	Hour	Summary of Events and Information	Remarks and references to Appendices
YPRES AREA	Aug. 1917			
	21st		B. Coy. took over work of forming track forward from PILCKEM ridge to LANGEMARCK along old roads.	
	22nd		A and C. Coys. continued work on GREEN LINE and D.Coy. on track. Wire spindles carried by Pack mules of Batt. Transports. Lewis Gun posts established on night of 22nd under command of Lieut DUNCAN. for anti aircraft work against low flying enemy planes over front lines on STEENBEEK and GREEN LINE 3 posts each.	2 OR Killed
	23rd		C. Coy. continued trench improvement and wiring on GREEN LINE. pack mules carrying munitions. A. Coy. commence duckboard track along Antwerp German Tramway from CANDLE TRENCH at C.5.9.6 past C.3.a.7.1.6 C.3.b.4.9. when Antwerp Tramway joins deep trench running parallel to DAVIES Rd in conjunction with 151 Field Coy. RE	Ateliers later. 3 OR wounded.
	24th		do do do	1 wounded

WAR DIARY
or
INTELLIGENCE SUMMARY. 19TH (PIONEER) WELSH REGT

Army Form C. 2118.

(Erase heading not required.)

Place	Date	Hour	Summary of Events and Information	Remarks and references to Appendices
YPRES AREA			AUGUST-	
	25th		A Coy. on Sunken Tramway. C.Coy. wiring the on GREEN LINE. D. Coy. Making track on road PICKEM-LANGEMARCK (2 O.R. wounded).	
	26th		Do. do. do.	
	27th		A and D Coy arranged to cooperate on clearing repairing put for artillery the road DAVIES ST. from IRON CROSS to LANGEMARCK. C. Coy to continue work on GREEN LINE. Parties detailed for day work & parties leaving in evening were unable to reach work owing to hostile barrages consequent upon the attack on EAGLE TRENCH.	
	28th		A and D. Coy. worked on DAVIES ST. First party leaving billets at am. Second party left 10am. clearing road filling in shell holes etc. Of First party 7 OR wounded (3 at duty). Of 2nd party 3 OR were laid low by C.Coy. continued wiring GREEN LINE. track of the were destroyed by shell fire & had to be replaced.	

Army Form C. 2118.

WAR DIARY
or
INTELLIGENCE SUMMARY. 19TH PIONEER BATTN WELSH REGT
(Erase heading not required.)

Instructions regarding War Diaries and Intelligence Summaries are contained in F. S. Regs., Part II. and the Staff Manual respectively. Title pages will be prepared in manuscript.

Place	Date	Hour	Summary of Events and Information	Remarks and references to Appendices
YPRES AREA	29th-30th		A and D Coy continued work on DAVIES ROAD + C Coy on GREEN LINE	
			A Coy hauled road slabs. Sband prepared artillery track across	
			two causeways across STEENBEEK. C Coy on wiring	
	31st		Do do D Coy + C Coy combined on chipping new lewis	
			GREEN LINE Casualties L.O.R wounded	
			During the month B Coy continued work of laying & maintaining	
			60 cm. railway under orders of A.D.L.R.S. Moved on 1st Aug	
			to B 9 c. 8. 2. Shed 28. took over maintenance of L.R. to ELVERDINGHE	
			The 58th Labour Coy was attached and with assistance of this Coy B Coy	
			took over maintenance of all 14th Corps L.R. to PILCKEM RIDGE. working	
			principally in BOESINGHE area where time was frequently cut by hostile	
			shell fire. The camping ground shelled 29th Coy moved on 30.8.16	
			B. 15 d. 8. 2.	

Army Form C. 2118.

WAR DIARY
or
INTELLIGENCE SUMMARY. 19TH (PIONEER) BATT'N WELSH REGT
(Erase heading not required.)

Vol 22

22 of 3 sheets

Place	Date	Hour	Summary of Events and Information	Remarks and references to Appendices
YPRES AREA	SEPTEMBER 1917.			
	1ST		H.Q. and 3 Coys in CANAL BANK C19.a. O.3. B.Coy B15.d.8.2 Transport A17.z.4.8.	
			A.Coy forming back slab track railway from Artillery STEENBEEK and DAWES St junction.	
	2nd		Cos'd D.Coy. Digging fire trenches and wiring on GREEN LINE	
			B.Coy on maintenance of 60 c.m. gauge light railway.	1. O.R. wounded
			A.Coy. d° d°	
			C & D Coys d° d° L.G. posts on GREEN LINE (3) and STEENBEEK (3)	
			maintained personnel relieved every 3 days	
	3rd 4th		D° d° d°	4. O.R. wounded 4"
	5th 6th		D° d° d°	3. O.R. wounded 8"
	7th 8th		D° d° d°	1. O.R. wounded 8"
	9th		Battn. move to PHEASANT CAMP PROVEN by train from ELVERDINGHE	
		1.30 A.M.	STATION. B.Coy joined at Station. Transport by road. Roll	
			call and still fire in neighbourhood of Station our shell fired	
			close to column	1.O.R. killed 2. O.R. wounded
			Capt. E.C. WALLACE R.A.M.C. K. attached M.O. to the Regt. struck down on way	

Army Form C. 2118.

WAR DIARY
or
INTELLIGENCE SUMMARY. 19TH (PIONEER) BATTN WELSH REGT
(Erase heading not required.)

Instructions regarding War Diaries and Intelligence Summaries are contained in F. S. Regs., Part II. and the Staff Manual respectively. Title pages will be prepared in manuscript.

Place	Date	Hour	Summary of Events and Information	Remarks and references to Appendices
	September 1917			
PROVEN	9th		Numerous occasions exceptional coolness dressing the wounds of the victims outside funk shells were falling in close proximity.	
			Batt arrived at PHEASANT CAMP. 3.15 pm	
	10th-11th		Paraded for inspection. Baths etc. 2nd Lt J.K.V. STEPHENS joined Batt.	appx 24
	12th		Batt moved by march route to billets in EECKE area (11 miles)	
	13th		d° d° d° to billets in MORBECQUE (9 miles)	
BAC ST MAUR	14th		d° d° d° to billets in BAC ST MAUR. (9 miles)	appx 25
	15th		Batt settled in billets. Fatigue parties furnished for R.E. Park & road mending on lent Rway. 2nd Lt W.H.Phillips and 74 O.R. were detailed to take over Rly Tramways on 16th Stack pier at D Coy billets.	
	16th		Rly Tramway system taken over. Party of 5 D.O.R. detailed to assist unloading —	
	17th		Rly Tramway system continued work 17th. Coal unloading.	
			Detailed 60 O.R. in 2 shifts to assist R.O.D. Bath Corps Siding on wagon lines. Major Roffey inspected site of trench to be dug? in consultation with the Brit G.O.C. and C.R.E. sited the trench	
	18th		Major Roffey & Capt Richards recce'd the site —	

Army Form C. 2118.

WAR DIARY
or
INTELLIGENCE SUMMARY. 19TH (PIONEER) BATTN WELSH REGT.

(Erase heading not required.)

Instructions regarding War Diaries and Intelligence Summaries are contained in F. S. Regs., Part II. and the Staff Manual respectively. Title pages will be prepared in manuscript.

Place	Date	Hour	Summary of Events and Information	Remarks and references to Appendices
	SEPTEMBER 1917.			
BAC ST MAUR	19th		A Coy at work C.T. night defensive flank at N.1.3.&.0.	
Sheet 36 1/40,000			B. Coy. on Tramways - C. Coy. on Coal and Store unloading	
			D Coy. site of work on left defensive flank inspected.	
	20th		A. B. and C. Coys. d⁰. d⁰. D Coy Commenced at H.36.a.	
			197 O.R. of 1st & 2nd London Reserve Field Coys joined Battn and were posted to Coys. 194 O.R. were transferred to Infantry. 100 to 10th Welsh & 94 to 14th Welsh Regt. Four L.G. posts for A.A. firing Established at ESTAIRES 2 at Bttº St MAUR	
	21st		A. C. & D. Coys d⁰ d⁰. Remainder of B Coy not employed on Tramways commenced work on left defensive flank at H.36a. just north of D Coy.	
			Capt. DONALD SEYMOUR JONES 4th R.W.F. joined Bn.	
	22nd		D⁰. d⁰. d⁰. 2nd LT. W.H. PHILLIPS appointed Divis.l. Tramway Officer.	
	23rd, 24th		D⁰. d⁰. d⁰.	
	25th		D⁰. d⁰. d⁰.	
	26th, 27th		D⁰. d⁰. d⁰.	
	27th, 28th		D⁰. d⁰. d⁰.	
	29th, 30th		D⁰. d⁰. d⁰.	

WAR DIARY
INTELLIGENCE SUMMARY. 19TH PIONEER BATTN WELSH REGT

Army Form C. 2118.

(Erase heading not required.)

Place	Date	Hour	Summary of Events and Information	Remarks and references to Appendices
BAC St MAUR.	Oct. 1917 1st		Four Coys employed on work in trenches. H.36.a and N.1.6 and N.2.6.	
			Detachment 1 Off. and 74 O.R. of B Coy on Trammways. L.G. fire mounted for anti aircraft shooting three Lewis Stores & Shops under construction	
	2nd 3rd 4th		do do do	
	5th 6th 7th		do do do	
	8th		do. During hostile air raid on Lund dropping near here made at O.R.C. St MAUR. caused 15 casualties Rank & W members were examined both wounded by Capt E.C.Wallace R.M.O. Major Hoysum left 16 Bn on route for Canada on leave	
	9th 10th 11th		do do do	
	12th		do do do	
	13th		do do do	
			do. 2nd Lieut G.E. Pritchard reported and was posted to C Coy. Chaplain J.P. Brooks Wesleyan Padre reported for duty	
	14th 15th		do do do	
	16th 17th		do do do. An O.R. 30.6.40 enemy shells 5.9 or 8ins calibre fell in BAC St MAUR. Some damage to houses	

Army Form C. 2118.

WAR DIARY
or
INTELLIGENCE SUMMARY. 19th (PIONEER) BATTn WELSH REGt

(Erase heading not required.)

Instructions regarding War Diaries and Intelligence Summaries are contained in F. S. Regs., Part II. and the Staff Manual respectively. Title pages will be prepared in manuscript.

Place	Date	Hour	Summary of Events and Information	Remarks and references to Appendices
BAC ST MAUR.	18th		Oct - Nov - 1917 -	
	18th		9 results and roof of Factory adjoining R.E. Park was pol on fire.	Lieut Capildio
SAILLY	19th 20th		Coys employed on work in trenches etc.	
	21st		Do do do Lieut C.J.S. NICHOLL and D.M. MORGAN joined for duty	
	22nd		Do do do H.Q. Mess Orderly Rm Signals etc. moved to billets in Rue des Trois SAILLY	
	23rd 24th		Do do do	
	25th 26th		Do do do	
	27th 28th		Do do do	
	29th 30th 31st		Do do do	

J. Dallin
Lt Col Comdg 19th Welsh Regt

J. Dallin Lt Col Comdg 19th Welsh Regt

Army Form C. 2118.

WAR DIARY
or
INTELLIGENCE SUMMARY. 19TH (PIONEER) BATTN WELSH REGT
(Erase heading not required.)

Vol 24

247
3 sheets

Place	Date	Hour	Summary of Events and Information	Remarks and references to Appendices
SAILLY.	1st Nov. 1917.		Four Coys employed on work in the trenches at H.30. N.2 and N.8 Sheet 36. Detachment of 1 Offr 74 OR on Tramways. 2 L.G. posts maintained at BAC. St MAUR. for anti-aircraft shooting. Erection of Horse Standings Work Shops etc at Transport Lines proceeding. C.6. Coy inspected & work to be taken over east of ARMENTIERES. B.Coy taken over work of C.Coy at.	
	2nd		Do do do. Advance party of C.Coy proceed to ARMENTIERES, to take over billets at H6.Z.6.8.	D Shoub reported
	3rd		Do do do. Remainder of C.Coy with transport and L.Gs. moved to ARMENTIERES to billets in COISNES Factory. RUE DE LA PAIX. H6.Z.8.9.	
	4th		Do do do do. C.Coy commenced work on drainage at C.28.d. and L.10.c. Hostile gas shelling interrupted progress	
	5th 6th		Do do do do	
	7th 8th 9th		Do do do do	
	10th 11th 12th		Do do do do	

Army Form C. 2118.

WAR DIARY
or
INTELLIGENCE SUMMARY. 19TH PIONEER BATTN WELSH REGT
(Erase heading not required.)

Instructions regarding War Diaries and Intelligence Summaries are contained in F.S. Regs., Part II. and the Staff Manual respectively. Title pages will be prepared in manuscript.

Place	Date	Hour	Summary of Events and Information	Remarks and references to Appendices
SAILLY SUR LA LYS	13th		Coys continues work as before. A Coy lost 1 Sgt. killed 2 men wounded	
	14th 15th		Do. do. do.	1 man wounded at duty. Shell
	16th		Message from 38th Div. stating that B. Coy is to be held in readiness to move.	A.B. Lanways 2Lt & Red. Adjut
	17th		Orders received for B Coy to proceed to entrain at LA GORGUE at 22 hrs 18th. Destination unknown. Coy under orders of the D.G.T.	
	18th		Capt. Bartlett takes over command of B. Coy, Capt. Austin of C. Coy. B. Coy entrains at LA GORGUE at 22 hrs. proceeding to report to A.D.L.R. 3.	
	19th		2Lt H.L. Davies commences duty as 38th D.T.O (in place of 2Lt W.H. Phillips who has proceeded with B. Coy.), with party of men from D. Coy.	
	20th		Remaining Coys continue as before.	
	21st		do do do	
	22nd		do do do	
	23rd 24th		do do do	
	25th		do do do	

Army Form C. 2118.

WAR DIARY
or
INTELLIGENCE SUMMARY. 19th PIONEER BATTn WELSH REGt
(Erase heading not required.)

Place	Date	Hour	Summary of Events and Information	Remarks and references to Appendices
SAILLY-SUR LYS	26th		News from B. Coy, stating that they Coy is working under A.D.L.R 3	D.B. Samways. 2 Lt & A/at Adj.
	27th		Wire from A.D.L.R 3 that location of B. Coy is ROISEL	
	28th 29th		C. Coy lost 1 O.R. killed in action	
	30th		Coys at work as before	
			do do do	
	1st			

Francis Dalton
Lt.Col. Comdg. 19th Welsh Regt.

Army Form C. 2118.

19 Welsh R.F.

Vol 25

WAR DIARY
or
INTELLIGENCE SUMMARY.
(Erase heading not required.)

Place	Date	Hour	Summary of Events and Information	Remarks and references to Appendices
H.Q. at SAILLY sur la Lys.	DEC. 1917.			
	1st		A. Coy. work in trenches CITY POST H.31. and HAYMARKET. B. Coy on Helachment under A.D.L.R. IIIrd Army. C. Coy working E. of ARMENTIERES on CONSETT AV. LOTHIAN and JABAN AV's. D. Coy working on concrete P.11 Box CITY RD C.T. and 1/2 Coy. detached under Divl Tramways Office 2nd Lieut H.L. DAVIES.	
	2nd 3rd 4th		Do Do Do	
	5th 6th		Do Do Do	
	7th		Do Do Do No 31855 Serjt E. Owen and 22196 Pte D. Bowen bth of C. Coy awarded Divl Certificates for their work on CONSETT Trench.	
	8th 9th		Do Do Do	
	10th		Do Do Do Transport Lines in RUE DES FIEFFS handed over to and of 2nd PORTUGUESE Divn. Transport moved to lines recently by 11th S.W.B. at FORT ROMPU.	
	11th		Do Do Do A and D Coys. handed over billets move to billets via H.10 near ERQUINGHEM. taking on work in GREATWOOD & FLEURIE SWITCH.	
	12th 13th 14th		Do Do Do Work of enlarging new horse standings commenced.	
	15th 16th 17th		Do Do Do Do Do carried on.	25 T 2 sheets

Army Form C. 2118.

WAR DIARY
or
INTELLIGENCE SUMMARY. 19TH (PIONEER) BN WELSH REGT

(Erase heading not required.)

Place	Date	Hour	Summary of Events and Information	Remarks and references to Appendices
H.Q. at SAILLY sur LA LYS.	18th Dec.		DEC. 1917. ARMENTIERES. Coys working in trenches continued.	
	19th		Do Do A. Coy. made responsible for FLEURBAIX defences	
	20th		Move of Coys and Transport A + D Coys. to old Billets in Rue du Quesnoy. G24.d.9.7. C. Coy from Armentieres bivouacked with A + D Coy for night. Transport to old lines G25.a.9.1.	
	21st		Completion of Move. C. Coy. to old billet G24.c.9.2. A. Coy. rest day.	
	22nd		A. Coy. resume work on C.T. N.2.c.1.3. C. D. Coy. rest day.	
	23rd		Do Do C. Coy take over work on GREATWOOD and CITY RD OLD CUT D. Coy. BOIS GRENIER CEMETERY POST. C. Coy take over defences of FLEURBAIX.	Artillery active [?]
	24th		Do Do Do No work in the line	
	25th		(Xmas Day.)	
	26,27,28 by 29.		Do Do Do A. Coy. Rest Day 24th. C. D. Rest Day 27th	
	30th		Do Do C. Coy. moves billets to BARLETTE FARM. B. Coy returns from work on Light R[ail]ways in neighbourhood of ROISEL and occupy billets vacated by C. Coy.	
	31st		Do Do Do	

M. R. J. Roffey Major

Army Form C. 2118.

WAR DIARY
INTELLIGENCE SUMMARY. 19TH (PIONEER) BATTN WELSH REGT

(Erase heading not required.)

Vol 26

Place	Date	Hour	Summary of Events and Information	Remarks and references to Appendices
H.Q. at SAILLY sur la LYS.	1st	TUES.	All Coys employed on work in forward area Map sheet 36. A Coy on C.T's at N1 and N2C. B Coy on GREATWOOD AV. OLD CUT and CITY? C Coy on defences around village of FLEURBAIX. D Coy on CEMETERY POST. FLEURIE SWITCH and concrete M.G. Pill Box at CITY POST. Detachment of D.Coy on Tramways 2nd Lt H.A.DAVIES. Dvl Tramways Offr. Regt Transport employed (carrying) Trawling material stores	Apps
	2nd		Do do do 2nd Lt F.W.NICHOLLS who reported 28.12.17 was returned on same date. Strength and posted to D.Coy the following officers who reported on same date were transferred under authority of G.O.C. Div 2nd Lt H.A. DAVIES and 2nd Lt G JENKINS to 15-13th Welsh Regt. 2nd Lt F. GIBBONS and 2nd Lt N. WHITEHEAD to 10 & 8th Welsh Regt. Capt W.A.RICHARDS -	Apps B
	3rd Wed		Do do do A. Coy Rest Day	
	5th		Do do do C and D Coy Rest Day	
	7th 8th & 9th		Do do do	
	10th		Do do do MAJ. M.H.ROFFEY, & ENGLAND. For transfer to TANKS CORPS.	

Army Form C. 2118.

WAR DIARY
or
INTELLIGENCE SUMMARY. 19TH (PIONEER) BATTN WELSH REGT
(Erase heading not required.)

Instructions regarding War Diaries and Intelligence Summaries are contained in F. S. Regs., Part II. and the Staff Manual respectively. Title pages will be prepared in manuscript.

Place	Date	Hour	Summary of Events and Information	Remarks and references to Appendices
H.Q. at SAILLY sur la LYS.	JAN. 1918 - ARMENTIERES.			
	11th Thurs		Work as before continued. Capt J.P. EMETT comdg Battn (Lieut Col R.GRANT-DALTON on leave to ENGLAND 21/12/17 - 20/1/18) Arr. Enby Reed Army	A673.
	12th		Do do do A and B Coys Red Day.	
	13th		Do do do C and D Coys Red Day.	
	14th		Do do Os.C. B and D Coys show arrangt. day billets to O.C. Coys of 5th NORTHAMPTONSHIRE REGT. T.O. shews 7 Lines etc. prior to handing over. Relief of 2 Coys 7th B. arranged for 17th inst	O.873.
	15th		Do do do Corr of blister moves to G.O.C. 12th Div 9.30 am. H.Q. 38th Div	O873.
			Transferred to MERVILLE Capt E.C. WALLACE M.O. i/c A.G.S. attached sick to 37th Field Ambulance.	
			The following officers mentioned in dispatches of 7.11.17 L.G. 21.12.17 Capt. & Adjt O.D. BLACK. Maj. R.B. HARKNESS. Maj. M.H. ROFFEY. Lt. J.H. JENKINS. O.R. Ranks 24220. C.S. Major McCarthy D. 3/886. Cpl. Q.M. Sergt Jenkins W.	
			Awarded D.S.O.- Maj. M.H. ROFFEY.	
			M.C. Capt. E.C. WALLACE R.A.M.C. attd.	O.S.13.

Army Form C. 2118.

WAR DIARY
or
INTELLIGENCE SUMMARY. 19TH (PIONEER) BN WELSH REGT
(Erase heading not required.)

Instructions regarding War Diaries and Intelligence Summaries are contained in F. S. Regs., Part II. and the Staff Manual respectively. Title pages will be prepared in manuscript.

Place	Date	Hour	Summary of Events and Information	Remarks and references to Appendices
H.Q. at SAILLY	JAN. 1918.		ARMENTIERES.	
	16th		Work as before continued. Capt. E.C.WALLACE. M.C. R.A.M.C. to hospital sick.	
Sm.GL.XS	17th		H.Q. less transport. B and D Coys. move to Lillers at NOUVEAU MONDE, rest of 5th Battn. Northamptonshire Regt. Pioneers. B and D Coys take over wiring behind Support Line. 2 Sections 87th Field Coy. R.E. pctd. D Coy. for work on M.G. Shelters. A & C Coys remain carrying on work on rifle defences "Haymarket" and FLEUR BAIX defences respectively. Regt Transport hauling R.E. stores from XV Corps Park and LA BOUDRELLE. 19th Ord. Park Office Reinforcements reported and posted as follows.	
			2nd Lieuts. I.K.GRIFFITH and R.O.PRICE to A.Coy.	
			2nd Lieuts. FREDERICK J. PARCELL and J.H.G. VAUGHAN to B.Coy.	
			2nd Lieutenant T.H.TILBY. to C.Coy. Capt.C.J.B.BUCHAN. R.A.M.C. joined as M.O.	
	18th		2nd Lieut. T.G.GREEN and J.L.RODERICK to D.Coy.	asfs
			C. Coy. handed over responsibility for renewing FLEUR BAIX defences to 6th 13th The Buffs at 4.30 p.m. Red Day for Barrack A and C Coys.	
			Baths at BAC ST MAUR not available owing to floods.	asfs
	19th		Red Day for B. and D. Coys. Baths still not available.	asfs

A6945. Wt. W14422;M1160 35,000 12/16 D.D.&L. Forms/C./2118/14.

Army Form C. 2118.

WAR DIARY
or
INTELLIGENCE SUMMARY. 19TH (PIONEER) BATTN WELSH REGT

(Erase heading not required.)

Instructions regarding War Diaries and Intelligence Summaries are contained in F. S. Regs., Part II. and the Staff Manual respectively. Title pages will be prepared in manuscript.

Place	Date	Hour	Summary of Events and Information	Remarks and references to Appendices
H.Q. at NOUVEAU MONDE	JANUARY 1918.			
	20th		Work in Trenches. Wiring and Concrete shelters for M.G. continued	O.T.B
	21st		Do do do Motor Lorries delivered material for B and D Coys.	
			Regtl Transport continued hauling for A and C Coys.	
			Lt Col D GRANT-DALTON returned from leave previous Coy	O.T.B
	22nd		Do do do	O.T.B
	23rd		Do do do Offrs & 2 sections 97th Field Coy R.E. withdrawn. Work of Concrete shelter construction taken over by D.Coy.	O.T.B
			B Coy taken over all wiring.	
	24th		Work continued as last stated	
	25th, 26th, 27th		Do do do A. C. Coy Rest Day 25th B.&.A.Coy Rest Day 26th B. Coy Rest Day all 26th	O.T.B
			at BAC ST MAUR. D.Coy arrived all 26th	
	29th		Do do do B Coy supply party left off loading stores from	
			trains on Rway BAC ST MAUR. Same for D Coy.	
	30 & 31st		Do do do Work commenced by D Coy on No 2 Concrete Shelter 30th	O.T.B
			A & C Coy Rest Day 31st No 1. Shelter complete. Lin and walls nearly covering	

Frank Dalton Lt Col
Cmg 19th Welsh Regt

WAR DIARY
INTELLIGENCE SUMMARY. 19TH (PIONEER) BATTN WELSH REGT

Army Form C. 2118.

Place	Date	Hour	Summary of Events and Information	Remarks and references to Appendices
H.Q. at NOUVEAU MONDE	FEB. 1918. ARMENTIERES.			
	1st Friday		All Coys employed on work in forward area Map Sheet 36. A. Coy on C.T. on right defensive flank of Bnt. Area (12th Divn) and C Coy on defences of FLEURBAIX under C.R.E. 12th Divn. B. Coy re-wiring behind support lines & furnishing carrying parties for D. Coy on ferro concrete M.G. Shelters. No. 1. Shelter complete. No. 2 at G.30.b3.9. nearing completion.	
			C.R.E XV Corps Troops. Right Transport Trenching slows.	P.T.O.
	2nd		do. do. do. Capt J.P. EMETT proceeded on 30 days leave. A & C Coys Rest day. 3rd Coy Rest Day leave 3/2 to 5/2	W.D.R.
	3rd		do. do. do.	
	5th		do. do. do. Capt WAR RICHARDS returned from 30 days leave	
	6th		do. do. do. Major R.B. HARKNESS rejoined from leave to CANADA. Following draft from 16th Welsh posted to this 19th joined. C.R. Lieut. T.H. JOHNS. 2nd Lieut G. ### F. FROOM, W.H. BRACE, W.G. CRIPPS	O.375 O.348
			R.P. TRUEBLOOD and W.E. DOWDING " and 135 O.R. (150 posted) 2nd Lieut. E.M. JONES and C.M. LLOYD posted but not joined	O.348 257F Attack

Army Form C. 2118.

WAR DIARY
or
INTELLIGENCE SUMMARY. 19TH (PIONEER) BATTN WELSH REGT
(Erase heading not required.)

Place	Date	Hour	Summary of Events and Information	Remarks and references to Appendices
	FEB. 1918.			
	6th	and	Battn remains attd 115th Inf Bde Staff.	
	7th & 8th		Work continued as previously stated. A and C Coys Rest Day on 8th	
	9th		Do. Do. Do. B and D Coys Do	O.O.T.B.
			2nd Lt. C.R.FROOM. rejoins 16th Welsh. Capt. E.E. KING posted to this Battn but remains attd 115th Inf Bde Staff.	
	10th & 11th		Do. Do.	O.O.T.B.
	12th		Do. Do. Coy Commdr of 2/5th L.N. Lancs. Look over work & billets prior to relief.	
	13th		Do. Do. A and C Coys Rest Day & bathed. Coy Commdr & Lookover billets of 2/5th L.N. Lancs & 57th Batt Pioneers at ERQUINGHEM. prior to relief.	O.O.T.B.
	14th		Battn less Transport Lines QM stores & Shops move to ERQUINGHEM in relief of and relieved by 2/5th N.L. Lancs (Pioneers)	O.O.T.B.
	15th		Took over A. C & D. Coys. Work on L'ARMEE LINE digging trenches & revetting. B. Coy in reserve for work for 114th Inf Bde. Are temporarily employed on sanitary work in village. A. C. Rest Days.	O.O.T.B.

Army Form C. 2118.

WAR DIARY
or
INTELLIGENCE SUMMARY.
(Erase heading not required.)

Place	Date	Hour	Summary of Events and Information	Remarks and references to Appendices
	16th		Work continued as last stated. B.Coy. work reconnoitred. 8 O.R's wounded - Shell. Casualties 1.O.R. wounds - Shell.	O.D.73.
	17th		Do. do. do. B.Coy. move to billets in Armentieres.	
			Reorganisation Instructions Authority War Office Letter No. 121/France/1588 (S.D.2) of 6.2.18 received	O.D.73.
	18th		A and C.Coy. work continued. B.Coy. commence work at MOURLINES.	
			Posts known as POPPY BANK, DURHAM CASTLE, CROSS CUT and HERRING POST. D.Coy work continued.	
			Conference of Coy Comd"s at 13th H.Q. reorganisation discussed. D.Coy to be disbanded.	O.D.73.
	19th		Work continued. D.Coy paraded at 2pm addressed by Comdg Offr afterwards marching in 3 parties to join Coys to which posted.	
			C.Coy. move to D.Coy. billets in Factory ERQUINGHEM.	O.D.73.
	20th		Do. do. do. 3 Coys. C.Coy carry on D.Coy's work. Transport move.	
	21st		Do. do. do. Q.M Stores move from ERQUINGHEM to new Transport Lines at HOLLEBECQUE CAMP.	O.D.73.
	22nd		Do. do. do. A.Coy. move to JUTE FACTORY ARMENTIERES.	

WAR DIARY
or
INTELLIGENCE SUMMARY.
(Erase heading not required.)

Army Form C. 2118.

Place	Date	Hour	Summary of Events and Information	Remarks and references to Appendices
H.Q. at ERQUINGHEM	22nd contd		prior to taking over work constructing new line at C.27a.7.3 - C.27c.7.4 in conjunction with 124 Field Coy R.E. C. Coy working on defences in conjunction with 123 Field Coy R.E. Sections D ammn chiefly revetment with shrapnel. C. Coy's Road Party for Batln.	O.J.B.
	23rd		Work continued At B Coy's Road Party - factory. Surplus animals transferred to S.L.D. 8. L. D. Mules. 2/Pack mules transferred to 57th Div. Pioneer Bn.	OJB
	24th		Work continued as last stated. D.Col. D'Grant-Dalton, DSO attd. Command of Pioneer Bn C.Os at ROUEN (24th-28th). Major R.B. Parmiter Cmd 2nd Batn.	OJB
	25	26th	do do do During work ending 20th expenses of bridge trestles	
	27th	26th	In ERQUINGHEM 2 at ARMENTIERES were reconnoitred by C.Os. 3rd in C and Coy Commanders and disposition of force and L.G.s discussed and arranged. In work on L'ARMEE LINE horse shovels and a plough were used to great advantage.	OJB

R.B.Crutchley Maj
Comdt 19 th Welsh R4

Army Form C. 2118.

WAR DIARY
or
INTELLIGENCE SUMMARY. 19TH (PIONEER) BATTN WELSH REGT.
(Erase heading not required.)

Vol 28

Place	Date	Hour	Summary of Events and Information	Remarks and references to Appendices
H.Q. at ERQUINGHEM.	1st March.		All Coys. employed on defensive works in forward area. A Coy N.E. defences of ARMENTIERES. B. Coy. HOUPLINES SECTOR for left sides of ARMENTIERES. C. Coy. line of posts outer defences of East ARMENTIERES. Regtl Transport employed hauling material etc. B.Coy. baths.	
	2nd		Do. do. do. A and C. Coy. baths. Lt. Col. D'Grand. Dalton resumes Comd.	A.573.
	3rd		Do. do. do.	
	4th		Do. do. do.	A.217
	5th		Do. do. do.	
	6th		Do. do. do. H.Q. move to chateau house near river at B.29.d.9.9	A.573
	7th		Do. do. do. Capt. J. P. EMETT reporting from 30 days leave to England. Working party of A.Coy night of 7th–8th suffered 11 casualties (8 gassed 3 wounded & duty) due to sudden intense hostile bombardment with gas shells directed on the site of the work.	A.538
	8th		Do. do. do.	A.538
	9th		Do. do. do.	nothing

287
5 sheets

Army Form C. 2118.

WAR DIARY
or
INTELLIGENCE SUMMARY.
(Erase heading not required.)

Place	Date	Hour	Summary of Events and Information	Remarks and references to Appendices
ARMENTIERES.	MARCH. 1918			
	10th	Midn	Work continued as last stated. News received that enemy attack might develop. Battle surplus transferred to Transport Lines.	
	11th		Bridge head defences further reconnoitred and wire entanglements pushed on. Ammunition installed.	O.O.B.
	12th		Do. do. do.	
	13th		Do. do. do.	O.O.B.
	14th		Do. do. do.	
	15th		Do. do. do.	
	16th		Do. do. do.	O.O.B.
	17th		ERQOINGHEM shelled. Canteen + Stables vacated. Battle surplus returned. Their Coy. + H.Q.	
	18th		Work continued as last stated. Working party of A. Coy. heavily shelled on march. Casualties 2 O.R. wounded. 12. N.Y.D. gas.	O.O.B.
	19th		Do. do. do. There was heavy shelling near Coy. billets.	

Army Form C. 2118.

WAR DIARY
or
INTELLIGENCE SUMMARY.
(Erase heading not required.)

Instructions regarding War Diaries and Intelligence Summaries are contained in F. S. Regs., Part II. and the Staff Manual respectively. Title pages will be prepared in manuscript.

Place	Date	Hour	Summary of Events and Information	Remarks and references to Appendices
ARMENTIERES.	MARCH.1918.			
	20th		Work continued as last stated. Much enemy shelling of Armentières and environs including large proportion of gas shells during night of 20th/21st.	
			Capt. D.S. Jones 4th R.W.F.(attd) to Hospital sick.	O.228
	21st	Do. do. do. Shell gas drift from town assumed H.Q. & Coys.	
		4 a.m.	During forenoon in addition shelling from lighter guns. Heavy shells apparently from 2 guns were observed falling in neighbourhood of one of our batteries at B.30.c.4.8. Coy Billets at B.30.a.0.7 and B.29.b.6.2 and H.Q. at B.29.b.9.9. Men were withdrawn to a flank from A.Coy. Billet (B.29.b.6.2.) & from H.Q. towards their shelling ceased men returned to Billets.	
		About 4.30 p.m.	Some heavy guns reopened and at about 5 p.m. heavy shell (15 in) fell about 15 yards from H.Q. Mess - of 5-Officers in the Mess at the time two only were wounded, both slight. Maj. R.B. HARKNESS	O.225

Army Form C. 2118.

WAR DIARY
or
INTELLIGENCE SUMMARY.
(Erase heading not required.)

Instructions regarding War Diaries and Intelligence Summaries are contained in F. S. Regs., Part II. and the Staff Manual respectively. Title pages will be prepared in manuscript.

Place	Date	Hour	Summary of Events and Information	Remarks and references to Appendices
ARMENTIERES.	MARCH 1918.			
	21st Cont.d		and 2nd Lt. D.B. SAMWAYS. Lt. killed was much damaged unfit for further use. H.Q. moved to cellar in late Factory B.27.b.6.3. O.R. casualties 1 slightly commotion.	O.D.B
	22nd		Work cont.d as last states. A working party of C. Coy. on ground which had been shelled with gas previous night suffered casualties the following. Army evacuates N.Y.D. gas. 2nd Lt. G.E. PRITCHARD, 2nd Lt. W.G. CRIPPS. and a Total of 51. O.R.	O.D.B.
	23rd		Do. do. do.	
	24th, 25th		Do. do. do. B. Coy. withdrawn from work for 114th Bde and commenced work on trenches in L'ARMEE zone.	O.D.B
	26th, 27th		Do. do. do.	
	28th		All Coys. concentrate on wiring in L'ARMEE zone. supply of material being very short hampers progress. C.O. inspects floating bridge sample at R.E. PARK.	O.D.B.

WAR DIARY
INTELLIGENCE SUMMARY.
(Erase heading not required.)

Army Form C. 2118.

Place	Date	Hour	Summary of Events and Information	Remarks and references to Appendices
ARMENTIERES	MARCH. 1918.			
	29th		Cautionary orders to prepare bivouac at short notice received. Found C Coy carried out usual bathing parades and out and night working parties. Definite orders to move received. C.O. reconnoitred bridge sites with C.R.E.	O.T.S.
	30th		Sites for floating bridges over the LYS marked by tapes in accordance with C.R.E's instructions. Batt- move to MENEGATE CAMP starting 5 p.m. move completed 7 p.m. - being relieved by 34th Div- less R.E and Pioneers.	O.T.S.
	31st		Batt- move to billets in CAUDESCURE. Starting 10 a.m. move completed 4 p.m. March 12 miles. Dinners en route. Capt C.J.S. NICHOLL proceeded to British Museum attd. Portuguese Corps. H.Q.	O.T.S.

James Salter Lt Col
Cmd. 19th Welsh Regt

Army Form C. 2118.

WAR DIARY
or
INTELLIGENCE SUMMARY.   19TH (PIONEER) BATTN WELSH REGT
(Erase heading not required.)

P/35   JA 29

Place	Date	Hour	Summary of Events and Information	Remarks and references to Appendices
	APRIL 1918.			
GAUDESCURE	1st		Battn marched from billets 2 p.m. to CALONNE SUR LYS. entrained	O.O.
	2nd		at 5.40 p.m. detrained at DOULLENS 6 a.m. 2nd marched to	
			ROBEMPRE via BEAUVAL and TALMAS.	
	3rd		Rest in billets at ROBEMPRE	
	4th		Inspections. Orders to move received 11.30 a.m. Battn moved at	Oct 15
			1.45 p.m. to billets in WARLOY-BAILLON via HERISSART and	
			CONTAY arriving at 5.45 p.m.	
WARLOY.	5th		All Coys employed digging Fire trench on "Green Line" thro V.26.a.	
			V.20.c. and V.20.a. Sheet 57.D.	
	6th		Do do do	
	7th		Do do do Capt. F.C. AUSTIN returns from 30 days leave	O.O.8
	8th		Do do do Capt AUSTIN resumed command of C. Coy. Capt. THOMAS to	
			A Coy as 2 in C.	
	9th		Do do do Capt Thomas to H.Q. as 2 in C.	
	10th		Orders for move received. Reconnaissance	TM
	11th		Capt. Richards to H.Q. as 2 in C. Capt Thomas to A Coy as O.C. Relieved 5th Northants	

29.7

Army Form C. 2118.

WAR DIARY
or
INTELLIGENCE SUMMARY.
(Erase heading not required.)

Place	Date	Hour	Summary of Events and Information	Remarks and references to Appendices
SENLIS	12th		In bivouac at V.10.b.0.3. Shelled out & established H.Q. at V.10.a.3.3. Shelled out during night.	Ptd
	13th		Established H.Q. at V.3 central, near C Coy. A & B Coy at V.10.a.5.5. Coy worked on Corps line. Night Work. Stand to 4.45 A.M daily.	Ptd
	14th		Coy continued work - Brews & Works. Battle Surplus Photographs to T. Hughes last photograph to Capt Mesgough. 50 (R) A Cy	
	15th		do	Ptd
	16th		do 1 OR killed 1 OR wounded (mounted) (C. Cy)	
	17th		do	
	18th		do	
	19th		do 3 OR wounded on work (C. Cy)	Ptd
	20th		do Infantry attacked front	
	21st		do	
	22nd		Ran Trench Digging & Returning for 113 Inf Bde. & operation. 1 O.R wounded	
	23rd		4th Coy Worke in front of our Trenches - 1 killed + 2 wounded (A. Cy)	Ptd
	24th		Coy moved to Camp at HERISSART.	

Army Form C. 2118.

WAR DIARY
or
INTELLIGENCE SUMMARY.
(Erase heading not required.)

Place	Date	Hour	Summary of Events and Information	Remarks and references to Appendices
HERISSART	25th		Bn moved back at short notice to Bivouac at V.3 central (SENLIS)	T.B.l.
SENLIS	26th		Orders received to move back to Camp at HERISSART on the 27th	T.B.l.
HERISSART	27th		Bn moved into Camp at HERISSART, letter of congratulation received from Div. Genl. ref work done by the Bn on nights of 22nd & 28th.	T.B.l.
	28th		C. of E. Church Parade.	
	29th		Paraded & Worked on protection of tents against bursting bombs.	
	30th		Move orders to return to forward area received on May 1st	T.B.l.
			3.5.18.	

Thomas Dalton Lt Col
Cmdg. 19th (S.) Bn. The Welsh Regt.

Copy

SECRET.

38th. Division No.S.S. 195/6.

19th. Welsh Regt.
(Glamorgan) Pioneers).

     The General Officer Commanding wishes me to place on record his appreciation of the good work done by your Battalion during the operations on the evening of the 22nd.inst. and again the following evening.

     The work of consolidation carried out by your Battalion materially assisted the Infantry in driving back the two counter attacks which were delivered by the enemy on the evening of the 23rd. and morning of 24th.

     An exceptionally long night's work was done by the party on the night 23rd./ 24th. owing to orders which were given to them on the spot to work on burying the dead after completing their task of consolidation; this very necessary, but sometimes thankless work of clearing the battlefield, was well carried out.

(Signed) J.E.Munby,
Lieut. Colonel
General Staff, 38th.(Welsh) Division

26-4-18.

Army Form C. 2118.

WAR DIARY
or
INTELLIGENCE SUMMARY.
(Erase heading not required.)

10th Welsh Regt (G)

Nov 30

Place	Date	Hour	Summary of Events and Information	Remarks and references to Appendices
SENLIS	1st		Bn. returned to Bivouac near V.3. central. Relieved 19th N.F. (35th Div. front) Remainder of Butts Surplus (7 Offrs 30 O.R.) proceeded to 38th Div. Depot at DOMQUEUR	
	2nd		Reconnoitring & commencing of work on ENGLEBELMER – BOUZINCOURT system of defences.	
	3rd		Reinforcements 3 Offrs 70 O.R. (Lt Paton, 2nd Lt Fagan + Jenkins)	
			Change of Coy names of Work – smaller area – Front Reserve BOUZINCOURT.	TM/
	4th, 5th		Coy continue BOUZINCOURT DEFENCES.	
	6th		A + B Coy. detailed for special task under 114 Bde. 2 O.R. wounded	
	7th		C. Coy on special work in AVELUY WOOD. A + B in reserve.	TM/
	8th		Rest of C. Coy on work. A + B told in reserve for operation. Congratulatory letter received from O.C. 15 Welsh on excellent work done by C. Coy on the 7th – preparation for operation – cutting of rides in AVELUY WOOD.	
	9th		A + B Coy proceeded to Assembly Post in the Wood ready for operation (114 Bde) on morning 10th. C. Coy on ordinary work.	M/

Army Form C. 2118.

WAR DIARY
or
INTELLIGENCE SUMMARY.
(Erase heading not required.)

Place	Date	Hour	Summary of Events and Information	Remarks and references to Appendices
SENLIS	10th		114th Fld Coy Operation took place. A & B Coys Parties in command of the 2 Coys. Frontal Hystevia attended. Capt McDONOUGH.	
			1 Offr Wounded = 2 Lt. E. GRIFFITHS, B Coy, 1 Offr Wounded (M. Duty) Cemetery	
			CAPT. M. P. McDONOUGH M.C. O.R. — 7 Killed 1 died of wounds	
			32 wounded 7 wounded (M. Duty) 1 to A.D.S. (N.Y.D.) 2 Missing	STA
			C. Coy on ordinary work 9 Offr 19 O.R. arrived from Battle Surplus.	
	11th		11 Offr 23 O.R. proceeded to join Battle Surplus (3R. Fw. Wing.)	STA
			A.B.& C. Coys continued ordinary work on eighty 11."	
	12th		2 Missing men found. — at R. Post. Work as usual.	STA
	13th		Work as usual — on Thypleheliner - Bony, enemy lines. 1 O.R killed 3 wounded	
			1 O.R. wounded at duty. (see A. Coy).	STA
	14th		46 Reinforcements from Pion. Bn. Work as usual.	STA
	15th		Coy on work as usual. Battle Surplus reliefs arrived from Div. Wing. 13 Grnades rejoined	
	16th		Relieved personnel proceed to Div. Wing. C. Coy were from V3c, to V16d.	STA
	17th 18th 19th		Coy on rest as usual	STA
	20th		Relieved by 19th N.F. and proceeded to camp at HERISSART. Bn. moved to Bivouag at V13c. to V16c., to work. under C.E., V Corps.	STA

WAR DIARY
or
INTELLIGENCE SUMMARY.

Army Form C. 2118.

(Erase heading not required.)

May.

Place	Date	Hour	Summary of Events and Information	Remarks and references to Appendices
HERISSART	21st		Bn. (less B Coy) in training at HERISSART	OTB1
	26th 27th		Bn. attached 115th Bde. Group, inspected by G.O.C. V. Corps.	
	28th		Training continued. B Coy still at work in SENLIS area	OTB1
	30th 31st		Bn. Sports & Shooting Competition held	

Edward Dalton Lt-Col.
Comdg 19th (P) Bn
The Welsh Regt.

WAR DIARY
or
INTELLIGENCE SUMMARY.
(Erase heading not required.)

Army Form C. 2118.

19th Welch (Pioneers)

95 31

817
2 shells

Place	Date	Hour	Summary of Events and Information	Remarks and references to Appendices
HERISSART	1st		June 1918 L.G. TEAM. won 1st Prize M.G. C.O. won 1st Prize Revolver Shooting	
	2nd		MAJOR F.R. DALE (R.W.F.) joined as 2nd in Command	
	3rd		Church Parade	
ENGLEBELMER	4th		Bn. marched to VARENNES (evening)	
	5th		Bn. marched to Bivouac P.30, P.36, Q.19, relieving 14th Worcesters (63rd Div. Pnrs)	
	6th 7th 8th 9th		Commenced work on Phythian Line. 7 hrs casualties 2 wounded (C. Coy) (A. Coy) Work continued	
	10th		Work as usual. 1 O.R. wounded (C. Coy)	
	11th		H.Q. moved from P.30 central to P.36a.1.9. 2 O.R. (C. Coy) wounded	
	12th–18th		Work as usual — Trench digging and wiring on Intermediate System	M.S.
	19th		1 O.R. B. Coy. 1 O.R. C. Coy wounded	
	20th		1 B wounded	
	21st 22nd		do do do	
	23rd		1 O.R. B. Coy wounded. Battle surplus exchange began	
	24th		Work as usual	

WAR DIARY or **INTELLIGENCE SUMMARY**

Army Form C. 2118.

19th Welsh (Pioneers) June 1918

Place	Date	Hour	Summary of Events and Information	Remarks and references to Appendices
ENGLEBELMER	25th		A Coy working on CLARENCE AVE. 2 O.R. (1 Coy wounded (4ws)	
	26th 27th		Work as usual. All Coys detached for work on CUTHBERT & CLARENCE AVs	
	28th		All Coys working CUTHBERT & CLARENCE AVs. 10.R. B.Coy wounded (4ws)	
	29th		do do do do 10.R. B.Coy wounded (4ws)	
			3 O.R. B.Coy wounded (1 died of wounds).	
	30th		Cmdg Off. appointed Acting C.R.E. 38th Divn. Work as usual.	JH1

M Dale Major
Cmdg 19th Welsh Regt

WAR DIARY
or
INTELLIGENCE SUMMARY

Army Form C. 2118.

19th Welsh Regt. (Pnr) 327

Place	Date	Hour	Summary of Events and Information	Remarks and references to Appendices
MESNIL SECTOR	1/7/18		HQ & A,B,C Coy in MESNIL SECTOR. — Work as usual. Transport lines at VARENNES — Lt Col D Grant-Dalton DSO appointed A/CRE. 38th Div — Major F.R. Dale cmdg 19th Welsh Regt — Capt K.S. Thomas acting 2nd i/c C.	
"	2/7/18		Work as usual — 1 O.R. accidentally injured	
"	3/7/18		Ditto — Capt W.R.R. Richards struck off strength classified B	
"	4/7/18		Ditto	
"	5/7/18		Ditto	
"	6/7/18		Ditto	
"	7/7/18		— Commenced work on QUAKER	
"	8/7/18		Ditto	
"	9/7/18		Ditto	
"	10/7/18		Ditto	
"	11/7/18		Ditto — Lt T.H. Johns, 2/Lt F.A. Froom, R.O. Price, F.W. Shea & G.K. Vaughan, O Jenkins proceeded to join 9th Batt Welsh Regt	
"	12/7/18		Work as usual — Lt Col D Grant-Dalton DSO appointed C of or 38th Div Works Officer	
"	13/7/18		Ditto — Rear H.Q. established at No 11 Billet LEALVILLERS.	
"	14/7/18		Ditto	

Army Form C. 2118.

WAR DIARY
or
INTELLIGENCE SUMMARY. 19th (P) Bn. The Welsh Regt.
(Erase heading not required.)

Place	Date	Hour	Summary of Events and Information	Remarks and references to Appendices
MESNIL SECTOR	15th		Weather Usual. 2. O.R. A. Coy wounded.	
"	16th	"	1. O.R. Wounded. Sgt. B. Coy.	
"	17th	"	Lt. S.M. Williams joined from 14th Welsh.	JTW1
HERISSART	18th	"	Bn. marched to HERISSART for training. HERISSART bombed by E.A. - 1 horse wounded.	
"	19th, 20th, 21st	"	Training programme carried out. Infantry Training.	
"	22nd	"	Training continued. Lt. H.L. DAVIES to England for TOUR of DUTY.	
"	23rd, 24th, 25th	"	"	
"	26th - 30th	"	"	
"	31st		MAJOR. R.B. HARKNESS reported from Base, rejoined the Bn., + assumed duties as 2nd in C.	JTW1
				1/18.
				8/18.

Bryan Dutton Lt. Col.
Comdg. 19th Welsh Regt.

Army Form C. 2118.

WAR DIARY
or
INTELLIGENCE SUMMARY. 19TH (PIONEER) BATTN WELSH REGT

(Erase heading not required.)

908 33 / 38

337 Hnhuck

Place	Date	Hour	Summary of Events and Information	Remarks and references to Appendices
HERISSART	AUGUST 1918.			
	1st & 2nd		Infantry Training continued.	
	3rd		Do. Do. Sports. 1st Prize High Jump won by Corporal Mills of this Battn	
	4th		Do. Batt. Horse Show and Races. Divl Steeplechase 2 miles.	
			The Battn entry "BRIDGE IV" finished third, ridden by 2nd Lieut. F.L. PARCELL of this Battn. 14 starters.	O.C.
	5th		Orders received that B. Coy would hold the line on returning to the front, subsequently cancelled as it was ascertained enemy had retired from AVELUY wood across river.	
	6th		Battn returned to the line. H.Q. at V.3. central Map Sheet 57.D.A and C Sy 1/10. near SENLIS. B. Coy near ENGLEBELMER. Relieved 7th Yorks & Lancs.	
	7th to		Pioneers of 17th Divn (Lt Col. D. GRANT-DALTON proceeded on leave Maj. R.B. HARKNESS in comd) Coys employed on improving trenches - SAUCHIEHALL RESERVE - OLDHAM and QUEENS AVENUE and B. Coy digging new trench Q.25.b.6.Q.26.c.	O.H.S.
	14th			
	15th		Orders to stand by.	
	16th		Coys employed on repair of roads east of the ANCRE leading to the crossings.	

Army Form C. 2118.

WAR DIARY
or
INTELLIGENCE SUMMARY. 19TH (PIONEER) BATTN WELSH REGT

(Erase heading not required.)

Instructions regarding War Diaries and Intelligence Summaries are contained in F. S. Regs., Part II. and the Staff Manual respectively. Title pages will be prepared in manuscript.

Place	Date	Hour	Summary of Events and Information	Remarks and references to Appendices
H.Q. at V.3. central	17th–21st		ALBERT SECTOR. Clearing & repair of roads continued.	
	22nd		Do. do.	CDS.13
	23rd to		Anti aircraft precautions on east bank of the ANCRE. Coys. follow up the advance and repair the roads as follows:– A. Coy. ALBERT – ~~AUTHUILLE~~	
			BAPAUME as far as Div Boundary. B. Coy. AUTHUILLE – THIEPVAL	
			C. Coy. AVELUY – OVILLERS – X.9.a.8.8. and from X.8.6.6.7. to R.33.d.8.3.	CDS.14
			MA Shell S.T.P. Parties were also detailed to assist 151st and 123rd	
	25th		Field Coys R.E. in repair of crossings AVELUY and AUTHUILLE.	
BOUZINCOURT	26th		Coys moved forward to bivouac. and H.Q. to do in BOUZINCOURT.	CDS.15
BAZENTIN le PETIT	27th		H.Q. moved to bivouac west edge of BAZENTIN le PETIT wood – where B Coys	
			joined. A. Coy. to X.11.c.9.7. The Battn. less 1 Coy. ordered to relieve Infantry	
	28th		in Front Line at LONGUEVAL. A. Coy. to be employed on roads. order	CDS.15
			cancelled 3 p.m. Orders from C.R.E. 7p.m. taking Line of resistance from LONGUEVAL	
	29th		HIGH WOOD. in conjunction 2 sections 124th Field Coy R.E. work completed	
			3.30 a.m.	

Army Form C. 2118.

WAR DIARY
OF
INTELLIGENCE SUMMARY. 19TH (PIONEER) BATTN WELSH REGT.

Place	Date	Hour	Summary of Events and Information	Remarks and references to Appendices
BAZENTIN le PETIT	AUGUST 1918.			
	30th		Road repairs continued - A. Coy. on road BAZENTIN le PETIT — MARTINPUICH	
			B. and C. Coys. LONGUEVAL — FLERS road.	
			Transport moved to lines at X.10.C.2.4 near CONTALMAISON.	COA
	31st		Do. Do. Do.	

(R.B. Seabourn?) Major
Comdg. 19th Welsh Regt (Pioneers).

Secret

19th. WELSH REGT
(Pioneers)
OPERATION ORDER.

1. The 38th. Division will attack east of river ANCRE on night 23rd/24th. Aug. 1918.
Further particulars were communicated at C.Os. conference to-day.

2. Coys. will repair the following roads so as to take horse transport and subsequently if their condition permits, motor lorries.

"A" Coy. ALBERT - BAPAUME road from X.13 d.0.0. north-eastwards.

"B" Coy. AUTHUILLE - THIEPVAL road.

"C" Coy. AVELUY (W.11 d.7.7.) road through W.18 a. and b. – OVILLERS – X.8.b.6.7. – X.9.a.8.8. and also from X.8 b.6.7. to R.33 d.9.3.

3. When moving off to commence work on roads (in para 2) each Coy. will send 1 runner to H.Q. On arrival at the work and having established a Coy. H.Q. as message centre, each Coy. will send a second runner to H.Q.

4. Reports of progress will be sent to H.Q. every 3 hours on each ½ mile of road repaired.

5. Strength of party on each road and of any other parties on other work at the time will be sent by first runners.

6. 120 rounds per man S.A.A. and all necessary tools will be carried.
Haversack rations will be taken and full water bottles

7. Suitable sites for forward locations of Coys. will be chosen and map ref. submitted to H.Q.

O.D.Black, Capt. & Adjt.
19 th. Welsh Regt.

23.8.18.

WAR DIARY
or
INTELLIGENCE SUMMARY.

Army Form C. 2118.

19ᵗʰ (PIONEER) BATTⁿ WELSH REGT.

WR 34

Place	Date	Hour	Summary of Events and Information	Remarks and references to Appendices
BAZENTIN le PETIT.	1ˢᵗ	2ⁿᵈ	Work on preliminary road repair. A.Coy. LESBOEURS – MORVAL road. B.Coy.	
	3ʳᵈ		[H.Q. and Coys. LONGUEVAL – FLERS road. C.Coy. d°. and relieved A.Coy. 3ʳᵈ inst	
MORVAL			moved to MORVAL] on LESBOEURS – MORVAL – SAILLY-SAILLISEL road.	O.O. 19
	4ᵗʰ		2ⁿᵈ inst. Transport moved to BAZENTIN le GRAND	
			A.Coy. d°. d°. A.Coy. SAILLY-SAILLISEL – LE MESNIL en ARROUAISE road; with	
			1 platoon of B.Coy. remainder of B.Coy. on LONGUEVAL – FLERS road	
			C.Coy. PERONNE – BAPAUME road where training thro. Oui area.	O.O. 13
			U.14.c.1.0. to O.31.d.9.0.	
LA TRANSLOY.	5ᵗʰ		d° d° d° 1 platoon from each Coy. in camp to load transport for	
			prospective move — emptying. In forenoon some dead over	O.O. 19
			Lived near MORVAL. Batt- less Transport moved to bivouac	
			at N.35.b. south west of le TRANSLOY.	
	6ᵗʰ		Batt-rested. Transport moved to line north of DELVILLE WOOD.	O.O. 19
	7ᵗʰ		d° d°. Lieut. L. EDWARDS took over duties of O.C. details and P.R.I.	O.O. 19
			from Capt. J.P. EMETT. ordered to England.	
	8ᵗʰ 9 & 10ᵗʰ		d° d°. Capt. EMETT proceeded for tour of duty in U.K.	O.O. 19 & 20

Army Form C. 2118.

WAR DIARY
or
INTELLIGENCE SUMMARY.
(Erase heading not required.)

Place	Date	Hour	Summary of Events and Information	Remarks and references to Appendices
ETRICOURT.	11th		SEPTEMBER 1918. Batt moved to V.2.c. Transport to K.10.9.4 north of ETRICOURT.	
	12th		Coys. work on roads. A.Coy. EQUANCOURT – NEUVILLE. B.Coy. P.35 central. – NEUVILLE C.Coy. FINS – P.35 central.	O.T.B.
	13th 14th		Do. do. do. A.Coy. also work on FINS – METZ road.	
	15th		A and C Coys. assist 12th Field Coy. R.E. on construction of Adv. Bde H.Qrs.	O.T.B.
	16th		B.Coy. relaying light railway between FINS and HEUDECOURT in conjunction with 152nd Field Coy. R.E.	
	17th		Operations of 38th Divn. 18.9.18. Battalion Orders attd. C.Coy less 1 platoon were attached to 115th Inf. Bde. A.Coy. to 114th Inf. Bde. for consolidation of M.G. posts and trenches and positions gained. B.Coy. were responsible for light railway from W.2.c.5.3 to front line in W.5.c. Map sheet 57c.S.E. 1:20000. No.11. Platoon C.Coy. Comdd. 2nd Lt. S.H. ALLEN left Camp 10 am to report to B.Coy. M.G. 13th attd 113th Inf. Bde. No.9. Platoon (attd. 16th R.W.F.) + 12 Platoon (att. 16th R.W.F.) proceeded from camp 7.30 pm.	O.T.B.
			Lt. T.L. JONES. in cmd. of No.9. and Lt. R.M. SAMPSON of No.12.	
			A.Coy. No.1. Platoon att'd 13th Welsh. Comdt. Lt. LLEWELLYN. No.2 Platoon att.14th Welsh. Comdt. Lt. S.M. WILLIAMS. No.3. Platoon att.15th Welsh. Comdt. 2nd Lt. F.W. NICHOLLS.	

WAR DIARY
or
INTELLIGENCE SUMMARY.
(Erase heading not required.)

Army Form C. 2118.

Place	Date	Hour	Summary of Events and Information	Remarks and references to Appendices
			No Platoon in reserve - all moved from camp at 7.30 p.m. Capt L.S. Thomas in comd of A Coy. and Capt. F.C. Austin in comd of C Coy. moved to this Double Coy. H.Q. at 7.45 p.m.	A&B
			Zero 5.20 a.m. 19.9.18. No 11. Platoon (divided in half platoons each att'd to a section of the M. Gns.) N° 9 and N° 12. Platoons were unable to perform the tasks allotted as advance on this bn Left Bde front did not progress satisfactorily. All however performed usefl work and participated in the fighting. Lt. T.L. JONES was wounded a few minutes after zero. N°s 9-11. Platoons returned to Camp at 10.30 p.m. 19th and N° 12. at 1.0 p.m. 19th. Total casualties 10 O.R. wounded. 4 O.R. killed. 16. wounded.	A&B
			On right Bde front, advance progressed and the Pioneers did useful work in consolidating, advancing with the few waves of Infantry, participating in the fighting and assisting in holding positions won. N°1. Platoon under Lt T. LLEWELLYN participated in 2 attacks. Completed all tasks allotted and remained at the front line till 9 p.m. 19th arriving in Camp 1 am 20th. N°2. Platoon returned 6 p.m. 18th. N°3. The reserve Platoon which has been used to consolidate and hold the line returned at 9 am 19th and N°4 at 1 pm 19th.	A&B

Army Form C. 2118.

WAR DIARY
or
INTELLIGENCE SUMMARY.
(Erase heading not required.)

Instructions regarding War Diaries and Intelligence Summaries are contained in F. S. Regs., Part II and the Staff Manual respectively. Title pages will be prepared in manuscript.

Place	Date	Hour	Summary of Events and Information	Remarks and references to Appendices
			Night of 18th–19th 2 platoons B.Coy. Aug 4. M.G. emplacements and 2 posts in No Mans Land. 2nd Lt. F.J. PARCELL in Command and night of 19th–20th a party composed of 60. O.R. B.Coy. and 30. O.R. A and 30. O.R. C.Coy. Aug 2. Posts and bombing stop wired — in No Mans Land on 114 R4a found Capt. M.P. McDONOUGH M.C. in Com?	
21st			Batt— less C.Coy. rested in camp —	O.O.S.
22nd			d°. d°. Revd/Coy. employed at Div. H.Q. Following 2nd Lieuts. joined from Base for duty.— W.G. CRIPPS. G. JENKINS. W.M. HORNE and W. HUGHES —	O.O.S.
23rd			Coys. in Camp training — ½ A.Coy. working at Div. H.Q.	
24th 25th			d°. d°. d°. Lieut. R.S. PALMER rejoined for duty. 2nd Lieuts. R.H. PUGH.	
26th 27th			d°. d°. d°. O.H. WATKIN and W. ROBERTS joined for duty.	O.O.S.
28th			Battle Surplus of 7 Officers and 94 O.R. joined Reception Camp. Battn moved to Bivouac in valley S.W. of HEUDICOURT. Transport joined N. of SOREL LE GRAND	O.O.S.
			A and B.Coys. laid out a H.T. Track from W.14.a — X.19.c. from N.W. of HEUDICOURT to N. of EPEHY.	
29th			B. Coy. work under III Corps Forward Roads Officers forming Lorry Track	O.O.S.

Army Form C. 2118.

WAR DIARY
or
INTELLIGENCE SUMMARY.
(Erase heading not required.)

Instructions regarding War Diaries and Intelligence Summaries are contained in F. S. Regs., Part II. and the Staff Manual respectively. Title pages will be prepared in manuscript.

Place	Date	Hour	Summary of Events and Information	Remarks and references to Appendices
HEUDECOURT.	SEP.r 19 18.			
	30th		from MALLASSISE FARM via LITTLE PRIEL FARM and forward easterly as far as situation permitted - bivouaced night of 30th Sept - 1st Oct. and resumed work at dawn completing track for Horse Transport to F.1.a.5.9 at which point coys. came under enemy rifle fire. Coys. returned to Camps at 4.30 p.m. Casualties 1.O.R. gassed. Orders received for Lieut. Col. D. Grant Dalton to report to 5th Div. to take comnd. of 2nd Battn. W: Yorks. Regt.	Opt.Slan
Lt Col A W W

BATTALION ORDERS
624.
by Major R.B.Harkness

1. WORK.   "A" Coy. will commence work on the road from SAILLY-SAILLISEL to LE MESNIL EN ARROUAISE tomorrow morning.
   "B" Coy. will carry on with the road on which they are at present employed. Transport as usual will be ordered, if necessary.
   "C" Coy. to repair the Main Road from U.14.c.1.0. to O.31.d.9.0. for Double Motor Lorry Traffic. C.R.E. particularly wishes the mud to be scraped off the road.
   The following points will be observed in road repairing:-
   1. The mud is to be scraped from the metalling.
   2. All drains are to be opened up and cleared to their outlets.
   3. Road is to be crowned.
   4. All Shell-holes or depressions are to be dug out as per sketch, before filling with brick or metal.

   5. Shell-holes to be drained to the bottom, or, if impossible to drain, to be baled out before filling.
   6. When sleepers or any timber is put in a road, they must be laid across the road and firmly bedded and spiked down.

   All work that is done temporarily or permanently will be done with this end in view.(Unless it is a road that will only be used for a day and then abandoned). Should temporary work be necessary, shell-holes may be filled with broken timber, boxes, or cans. These can easily be removed and permanent work be done. If these holes are filled with earth it makes more work eventually. Instances may however occur where earth will have to be used. No road is to be reported fit for double H.T. or M.T., unless it is the proper width throughout.

2. BATTLE SURPLUS STRENGTH.

ARRIVALS. 1-9-18.   23928.Pte.JAMES,J.(C),58928.Pte.GEORGE,(A),
   32031.Pte.RUBERY,(B),60443.Pte.RICHARDS,(A). From leave

DEPARTURES. 2-9-18. 27141.Pte.HOWE,(C) Leave to U.K.

Blamway Lieut
for
Capt. and Adjt.,
19th. Welsh Regt.,

3-9-18.

OPERATION ORDER
By Lieut.Col.D.Grant-Dalton, D.S.O.,-

H & mess

1. At a date and hour to be notified later the Division will attack with limited objectives.

2. The attack will be carried out by 113th.Bde. on the left, and 114th.Bde. on the right. Limits of Bde.fronts have been notified to those concerned.

3. C.Coy.(less 1.platoon) will be attached to 113th.Bde.for consolidation of L.G. & M.G. positions. 1.platoon to 14th.R.W.F., 1.platoon to 16th.R.W.F., 1.Platoon to "B"Coy.M.G.Battn. Details have been notified to those concerned. 1. platoon to continue work in liason with 134th. Field Coy.R.E.

4. A.Coy.will be attached to 114th.Bde.for assistance in consolidation of objectives. 1. platoon to 13th.Welsh Regt., 1.platoon to 14th. welsh, 1.Platoon to 15th.welsh. 1.Platoon will be held in reserve at double Coy. ~~xxxx~~ Adv.H.Q. Details have been issued to those concerned.

5. Advanced Coy.H.Qrs.for A.and C.Coys.will be at **W.3.a.4.1.**

6. On completion of tasks, Platoons will rendezvous under Platoon Commanders, and report such completion to their respective Infantry Battalions to which attached. They will also report by runner or otherwise to their Adv.Coy.H.Q. stating particulars of casualties & condition of work.

7. "B"Coy.will be responsible for the maintenance of the Tramway from W.2.c.5.3. to our present front line in W.5.c.For this purpose 1.platoon will be bivouaced at a convenient point, to be selected

W.7.a.8.2

by O.C."B"Coy. This maintenance work will be continued until the Coy. is relieved of the responsibility. The remaining platoons of this Coy. will work in liason with O's C.151 and 124 Fld.Coys.R.E.Details have been notified to those concerned.

8. Advanced H.Qrs.will be established as follows- 113 & 114th.Bdes.W.3.a.2.0.: 13th.,14th.& 16th. R.W.F. Q.34.a.9.5.,13th.,14th.,15th.,Welsh,W.4. a.05.40. Main Div.R.E.Dump,P.39.b.Adv.Div.R.E. Dump,W.3wb.3.3. Coffee Bar,V.11.a.9.9.: R.A.P's., (left) Q.33.central.(right) W.4.a.central. A.D. S.FINS V.11.b.0.8.

9. RATIONS.Those concerned in operations will carry the unexpired portion of the day's rations together with a portion of the hard ration for the following day. An issue of rum will be made to those ranks only directly concerned in operations.

10. TRANSPORT.T.O.will load 4 limbers to fullest capacity with wire concertinas.These loaded limbers to report to O.C."C"Coy. by 7-30 p.m. 17th.Instant.

11. Two H.Q.Cyclists will be attached to Adv. Coy.H.Q. for liason with Battalion H.Q.only. Battalion H.Q.will remain at its present location.

                          Capt. and Adjutant,
                            19th.Welsh Regiment,

17-9-18.

-BATTALION ORDERS-
638.
-By Lieut.Col.D.Grant-Dalton,D.S.O.,-

The Commanding Officer wishes to place on record his high appreciation of the gallant conduct and splendid endurance displayed by all Officers and other ranks engaged in the recent operations. The conduct of all was worthy of the highest traditions of British Infantry. Where all displayed the greatest courage, and many gallant acts remain unrecorded, the following ranks showed exceptional courage and determination in the execution of their duty:-

    56500. Sergt. AFFLEY, W.
    31961. " BRAIN, G.
    55893. Corpl. BLEASEDALE, E.
    32086. " BOLTON, C.F.
    60366. Pte. BOWYER, A.E.
   285383. " EVANS, J.C.
    76746. Corpl. HARDY, J.
    31651. L/C. HOLCROFT, T.
    55082. Pte. HOWELLS, A.
    43713. " HAWKINS, E.F.
    1452. " HARES, T.
    12318. " JONES, J.
    35313. " JONES, T.H.
    31857. L/S. LONG, W.
    54519. Pte. LLEWELYN, W.D.
    9319. Sgt. MORGAN, T.
    32087. Pte. MEEHAN, B.
    49750. " OWEN, D.S.
    60417. " PURKISS, J.
    31047. Sgt. WHITFIELD, J.

(Signed) O.D.Black, Capt. & Adjt.,
19th. Welsh Regiment.

20-9-18.

WAR DIARY
or
INTELLIGENCE SUMMARY
(Erase heading not required.)

Army Form C. 2118.
Vol 35 P/36

Place	Date	Hour	Summary of Events and Information	Remarks and references to Appendices
HEUDICOURT	1st		19th (P). Bn. The Welsh Regt.	
	5th		Bn resting. Infantry Training. Small party working on Div. H.Q. & C.R.E. H.Q., also constructing Range.	
	3rd		Lt.Col. D. GRANT-DALTON DSO left Bn on 3rd to take over command of the 2nd West Yorks. MAJOR HARKNESS in command - CAPT. L.S. THOMAS a/g 2 i/c.	
			Military. Following decorations + honours granted to the Unit for operations near GOUZEAUCOURT 17th – 21st Sept. Bar to M.M. 56500 Sgt AFFLEY. M.M. to Pte (A/Lcpl) T. HAYRES. Div. Certificate for gallantry to 32066 Cpl. BOLTON, F. 45745 Cpl. HARDY. J. 55823 Cpl. BLEASDALE. E. 2319 Sgt. T.G. MORGAN. 54519 Pte LLEWELYN. W. D. 49750 Pte OWEN. D.S. 55082 Pte HOWELLS. A.	
EPEHY	5th		B Coy immediately proceeded to work on approaches to bridges over canal at OSSUS. A. Coy working in tunnel.	
	6th		Coys continued work at OSSUS. B + C. Coy bivouacing near work at S.22.c. (near VENDHUILLE). C Coy continued work at OSSUS.	
	7th		Bn. moved into Bivouac at OSSUS.	
VENDHUILLE	8th		Coys working in tunnel through AUBENCHEUL, VILLERS-OUTREAUX	
	9th		Bn move to MALINCOURT. Coys working in roads to MALINCOURT.	

Army Form C. 2118.

WAR DIARY
or
INTELLIGENCE SUMMARY.
(Erase heading not required.)

October 1918.

19th (P) Bn The Welch Regt.

Place	Date	Hour	Summary of Events and Information	Remarks and references to Appendices
MALINCOURT	10th		A & B. Coy working on Roads from MALINCOURT to WALINCOURT. C. Coy building new Div. H.Q. near VILLERS OUTREAUX	JKG
	11th		Coy working on roads MALINCOURT - WALINCOURT	JKG
	12th		Bn moved to Billets at BERTRY	JKG
BERTRY	13th		All Coys on work, repairing & cleaning Rd. BERTRY - TROISVILLES & through NEUVILLY & LE CATEAU.	JKG
	14th		Coys on work as on 13th	JKG
	15th		Coys on work as on 14th	JKG
	16th		A & B on new Brigade Battle H.Q., on INCHY - LE CATEAU Road. C. Coy Engineers water pipes at BERTRY	JKG
	17th		Coys on work -do- as on 16th	JKG
	18th		All Coys on work making 2 new Brigade Battle H.Q. on INCHY - LE CATEAU Road. 1 O.R. D "A" Coy wounded. B/Dumps moved to BERTRY	JKG
	19th		B & C Coys prepared for operations - A Coy completed work of 18th	JKG
	20th		"B" Coy & ½ "C" Coy attached to 114th & 113th Brigades respectively, participated in operations on the "Le Cateau" sector, on the night 19th/20th. Consolidation & Polygiënic state by these Brigades was satisfactorily completed by our own platoons. Capt. M.P. McDonagh was in charge. Casualties :- 1 O.R. Killed. 13 O.Rs wounded. 1 O.R. M.V.D. Lce Cpl "A" Coy worked on apparatus & bridge in connection with	JKG

A6943 Wt.W14427/M1160 35,000 12/16 D.D.&L. Forms/C/2118/17

Army Form C. 2118.

WAR DIARY
or
INTELLIGENCE SUMMARY.
(Erase heading not required.)

October 1918

Place	Date	Hour	Summary of Events and Information	Remarks and references to Appendices
BERTRY	21st		"A" Coy + ½ "C" Coy on work repairing roads between NEUVILLY & LE CATEAU	1.O.R. 7 "B" Coy accidentally injured
	22nd		All Coys on work repairing & clearing roads & bridges around MONTAY	1 O.R. 7 "C" Coy accidentally injured
	23rd		All Coys resting	
	24th		Battn moved to bivouacs at K.16 near MONTAY. ½ Coy A ½ Coy C on work repairing MONTAY-FOREST road.	
MONTAY	25th		Battn moved into billets at VERT BAUDET (near FOREST) & CALUYAUX (near FOREST). ½A Coy & ½ C Coy worked on MONTAY-FOREST road	
CALUYAUX	26th			
	27th		Coys working on roads. A Coy on work on CALUYAUX-OVILLERS road; B Coy repairing road from PAVÉ JACQUES Fm to POIX-DU-NORD; C Coy repairing road through WARGNONVILLE. The following officers have been struck off the strength having been refuted to be following fighting units of the Div. CAPT C.J.S. NICHOLL - 16th R.W.F.; Lt B.L. PRITCHARD - 13th WELSH; Lt C.M. LLOYD - 10th S.W.B.; 2/Lt W.G. CRIPPS - 15th WELSH; 2/Lt G. JENKINS - 15th WELSH; 2/Lt O.H. WATKINS - 15th WELSH; 2/Lt W. ROBERTS - 13th WELSH.	
	28th		A Coy worked on ENGLE-FONTAINE road; B Coy repaired CROIX-CALUYAUX-VENDEGIES road	

WAR DIARY or INTELLIGENCE SUMMARY

Army Form C. 2118.

Month: October 1918

Place	Date	Hour	Summary of Events and Information	Remarks and references to Appendices
CALUYAUX	28th		C Coy repaired road at F.11.b.1.3 (Sheet 57ᵉ NE) 1/₄₀,₀₀₀ POIX-DU-NORD.	B.G.S
	29th		A Coy worked on road to POIX-DU-NORD. B Coy filled in craters. C Coy formed a new Coy HQrs Bay Track.	B.G.S
	30th		from FOREST to CALUYAUX. A Coy worked on road to ENGLEFONTAINE. B Coy filled in craters at ENGLEFONTAINE. C Coy completed Track. At 1800 hrs enemy heavily shelled cross roads near Coy billets; 1 OR killed, 11 ORs wounded, 1 OR M.D. Gas. Following decorations granted to the Unit for operations near MONTAY + Honours on the night of the 9th – 20th inst:- M.M. 47832 Cpl. F.T. DRAKE ; M.M. 23116 Cpl. H. GALE ; M.M. 31786 Pte O. EVANS	B.G.S
	31st		A Coy worked as usual. C Coy erected protective embankment against shell splinters at Transport lines.	B.G.S

31.10.18.

[signature] Lt.Col.
Commanding 19th (Pioneer) Bn. Welsh Regiment

SPECIAL ORDER OF THE DAY

by

Major General T. ASTLEY CUBITT, CMG., DSO.,
  Commanding 38th. (Welsh) Division.

Saturday, 26th Oct. 1918.

I desire to offer my most cordial congratulations to the Division on the brilliant feat of arms accomplished by them on the 20th instant.

I have personally, accompanied by many Senior Officers of the Division, traversed the entire battlefield, and I am once again lost in admiration at the gallantry and determination of the troops of this Division in surmounting the obstacles with which they were confronted.

You formed up in boggy ground, crossed a difficult river (for the fourth time since 21st August), attacked up a glacis swept by Machine Gun fire, stormed a precipitous railway embankment 40 to 50 feet high, and in pouring rain, very slippery and deep going, in the hours of darkness, established yourselves on the final objective punctually and to time.

Very strong opposition was encountered on the railway, also when consolidating on the final objective, but direction and distance were maintained throughout; this was especially noticeable on the right of our attack.

In particular I wish to tender my most sincere congratulations to Brigadier General H.E. ap RHYS PRYCE, CMG., DSO., Commanding 113th Infantry Brigade, and the 13th., 14th., and 16th. R.W.F., to Brigadier General T.R.C. PRICE, DSO., Commanding 114th Infantry Brigade, and the 13th and 14th. Welsh Regiment; to Lieut. Colonel R.B. HARKNESS, and his two companies of the 19th. Welsh Regiment (Glamorgan Pioneers) who, when the left of the attack was temporarily checked, charged through the attacking Infantry overcoming opposition on the railway, and consolidated on the final objective, capturing four field guns and accounting, with the bayonet, for their detachments complete; to Brigadier General T.E. TOPPING, CMG., DSO., C.R.A. and to Lieut. Colonel A.G. LYTTELTON, M.G. Battn. for their most carefully prepared and accurate gun and machine gun covering fire which enabled the Infantry to storm the railway embankment and gain their objectives; and especially to Lieut. Colonel T.E. KELSALL, DSO, C.R.E. and all ranks of the 38th Divisional Royal Engineers for their sustained gallantry and endurance under heavy shell fire, and nightly gas, which resulted in 24 Bridges being built over the SELLE River, thus enabling our Infantry and Artillery to cross and achieve the results sets forth above.

T. Ashley Cubitt.

26th October 1918.   Major General.
Commanding 38th.(Welsh) Division.

(Copy)

SPECIAL ORDER
By
Lieut. Col. R.B. Harkness, Commanding 19th Welsh Regt.

The Commanding Officer wishes to place on record his high appreciation of the gallant conduct and splendid endurance displayed by all Officers and Other Ranks of "B" and "C" Coys., during recent operations.

The G.O's. C. 113th and 114th Infantry Brigades highly appreciate the work done, and praise the conduct of all ranks whose gallantry contributed in no small manner measure to the success of the operations.

Special mention is made of the following O.R's who showed exceptional courage and determination in the execution of their duty:-

"B" Company.				"C" Company.		
206788	Sergt.	Harper E.C.		31745	Sergt.	Murphy M.
65322	"	Stephens C.		31575	"	Wilkins W.C.
30854	L/Sgt.	Greenland A.		53823	Corpl.	Bleasdale E.
47832	Corpl.	Drake F.H.		31540	"	Partridge W.
23116	"	Gale H.		31786	Pte.	Evans O.
32680	Pte.	Hill J.		31830	"	Parsons J.
31394	"	Harris F.		32093	"	Pickering W.
20075	"	Rolt T.		55755	"	Turley C.

(Signed) D.G. Davies,
Lt. & A/Adjt.
19th Welsh Regt.

21.10.18.

Army Form C. 2118.

19 Welsh
P 38

Vol 3
6

WAR DIARY
or
INTELLIGENCE SUMMARY.
(Erase heading not required.)

November 1918

Place	Date	Hour	Summary of Events and Information	Remarks and references to Appendices
CALUYAUX	1st		A Coy worked on temporary road near ENGLEFONTAINE; B Coy picked off elevations and cable at ENGLEFONTAINE; C Coy engaged on work at Temporary road.	DGW
	2nd		A Coy picked off Temporary road; B & C Coys resting	DGW
	3rd		A & C Coys engaged on making track from VERT BAUDET to ENGLEFONTAINE. This was completed ready for operations on 4th inst	DGW
	4th		A Coy worked on road ROUTE D'HECQ. C Coy reconnoitred & worked in conjunction with 1st Field Coy REs on roads in FORÊT DE MORMAL in connection with operations executed by 4th Corps on afternoon of 4th inst. B Coy in reserve	DGW
ENGLEFONTAINE	5th		Batt moved to ENGLEFONTAINE. Coys worked on roads in FORÊT DE MORMAL	DGW
	6th		Coys worked as usual	DGW
	7th		Batt moved to BERLAIMONT; A&C Coys did old work; B Coy worked on roads near LOCQUIGNOL	DGW
BERLAIMONT	8th		A Coy worked on AULNOYE – POT-DEVIN road; B Coy worked on Gate Valve or level crossing near AULNOYE STATION; C Coy worked on DOURLERS road	DGW
	9th		Coys worked as usual	DGW
AULNOYE	10th		Batt moved from BERLAIMONT to Factory at AULNOYE. Coys worked on roads	DGW
ECUELIN	11th		Batt moved from AULNOYE to farms in V.26 V.27 near ECUELIN. Coys worked	7.12. 36 7 sheets

Army Form C. 2118.

WAR DIARY
or
INTELLIGENCE SUMMARY.
(Erase heading not required.)

Month: November 1918

Place	Date	Hour	Summary of Events and Information	Remarks and references to Appendices
ECUELIN	11th		Coys worked on the DOULERS-FOURSIES-MATIGMIES road. At 1100 hrs hostilities ceased. Information was received that hostilities would cease at 1100 hrs	
	12		Coys worked as usual	
	13		Ditto	
	14		"	
	15		"	
	16		"	
	17		Coys rested. Congratulatory letter received from G.O.C. 38th Div. Allotted amount of B.W. Guard furnished by the Bn.	
BERLIAMONT	18th		Bn. moved to billets in BERLIAMONT	
	19th, 20th, 21st, 22nd, 23rd		Parade in the morning. Sports & Recreation in the afternoon. ditto	
	24th		Church Parade. Sgt. M. Murphy C. Coy. awarded D.C.M. for Gallantry in action	
	25th		Parades in morning. R.A.M.C. v. 19th Welch — Sports. Rugby. 7 Welch v. Rt. & Recovery	
	26th		Presentation of Ribbons by G.O.C. 38th Div. to Rt. & Recovery M.C. — Capt. ?/C. Austin M.S.M. — Sgt. T. Martin Bn. Coy. Cpl. Hayden Pte. Bottomley M.M. — Cpl. Wright, Cpl. Drake, Sgt. T. Hughes, Pte. Howells, Pte. McMurphy, Pte. Bleasdale	

Army Form C. 2118.

WAR DIARY
or
INTELLIGENCE SUMMARY.
(Erase heading not required.)

Army Form C. 2118.

19th (P.) Bn., The Welsh Regt.

November 1918

Place	Date	Hour	Summary of Events and Information	Remarks and references to Appendices
BERLAIMONT	27th		Parades. Gymp. R.E. Engrs. 19th W.R. v. R.A.M.C. Result Bralters Draw	
	28th		Parade in morning. Sports in afternoon	
	29th		Parade do do Gymp. R.E. Engrs. 19th W.R. v R.A.M.C. won 6th to 4lb	SS1
	30th		do do do Sports in Afternoon	SS1

L.S. Thomson, Major
Cmdg. 19th Welsh Regt.

Copy
Sent on to Corps 17-11-18

O. C.

<u>19th. Welsh Regt. (Glamorgan Pioneers)</u>

    The Divisional Commander desires me to express to you his thanks for the Guard at Divnl. H.Q. which has been found by your Battalion.

    At the same time he wishes me to tell you that he has been greatly pleased at their smart and soldierly appearance and the uniformly excellent manner in which they have carried out their duties, He considers it one of the best Guards which has been mounted at H.Q. since he commanded the Division and he is highly gratified to find that his Pioneer Battalion, in this respect as in others, does credit to the Welsh Division.

16th. November 1918.

Lieut. & A.D.C.
for
G.O.C. 38th. (Welsh) Divn.

Army Form C. 2118.

WAR DIARY
or
INTELLIGENCE SUMMARY.
(Erase heading not required.)

19th Welch

Army Form 37

603 377 1 sheet

Place	Date	Hour	Summary of Events and Information	Remarks and references to Appendices
CORBIE	1st – 10th		Bn continued with Parade at 9.30 a.m. daily – up to 2 hours. Sports in the afternoons; concerts and sing-songs in the evenings. Inter-Platoon competitions in Sports organised	AF/
	10th 11th 12th		Bn marched to ENGLEFONTAINE Bn entrained at SALESCHES. Transport proceeding by road. Bn arrived at VILLERS BRETONNEUX and marched into Billets – H.Q. & 2 Coy at CORBIE, A & C Coy at FOUILLOY	AF/
	13th & 14th		Bn engaged in kit Inspections etc. Personal Parties spread to new billeting area. Bn requirements sent to be done in preparation for arrival of drivers in this area	
ST GRATIEN	15th		H.Q. moves to ST. GRATIEN. 'A' to MOLLIENS, 'B' to ALLONVILLE 'C' to LA NEUVILLE CAMP.	AF/
	16th, 24th, 25th, 26th, 27th – 31st		Bn employed on preparation of Billets for 114 Inf. Bde. Holiday. Preparation of Billets for 114 Inf. Bde continued	

R.B. Hankinson
Lt Col
Comdg 19th Welch

19th Welsh
28 January 1919 F77

19th Welch Rd
19 Welsh Rd
F77
SS 38

WAR DIARY
or
INTELLIGENCE SUMMARY.
(Erase heading not required.)

Army Form C. 2118.

Place	Date	Hour	Summary of Events and Information	Remarks and references to Appendices
ST. GRATIEN	1st		Bn. continued with work on 114 Inf. Bde. Billets	H.Q.
	2nd		H.Q. moved from ST. GRATIEN to LA NEUVILLE CAMP. T. Lines " ALLONVILLE "	
LA NEUVILLE	3rd		B. Coy moved from Billets in ALLONVILLE to CARDONETTE going to occupy & dispense in this area. Bn now distributed — H.Q., T. Lines + C. Coy LA NEUVILLE CAMP B. Coy — CARDONETTE. A. Coy — MOLLIENS AU BOIS and BEAU COURT.	
	4th		Work on 114 Bde Billets continued	Billet improvements constructed of huts &c
	5,6,7		do do do do	
	8th		do do do do	
	9th	10th	do do do do	
	11th		do do do do	First batch other than miners — incl'g 2/Lt.Pictor left unit proceeding to concentration Camp SAVEUSE for demobilization	OTP S
	12th	13th	do do Lieut D.G. DAVIES and D.B. SAMWAYS proceed further parties	OTP S
	14th	15th	do do do 12th ret'd for demobilization also 2nd Lt W.M. HORNE & 2nd Lt T.H. TILBY proceeded for demob 15th	6309 OTP

GENERAL STAFF
38TH (WELSH) DIVISION
22-2-19

Army Form C. 2118.

19th Welsh Regt

WAR DIARY
or
INTELLIGENCE SUMMARY.

January 1919.

(Erase heading not required.)

Instructions regarding War Diaries and Intelligence Summaries are contained in F. S. Regs., Part II. and the Staff Manual respectively. Title pages will be prepared in manuscript.

Place	Date	Hour	Summary of Events and Information	Remarks and references to Appendices
LA NEUVILLE	16th		Work continued as before.	
			Presentation of Colours - Concentration of Colours - presented by H.M. The King - took place at ALLONVILLE. The Colours were received from the hands of the Major General Comdg. by Lieut. J. D. WALTERS, a representative party from H.Q. and each Coy. attended the Ceremony.	A.T.A.
	17th		Work continued - Dental Mess at LA NEUVILLE Camp was opened up to this date inclusive a total of 5 Officers and 444 O.R. in addition to Misses Zurn provided for Demobilisation.	A.T.A.
	18th		Work continued as before. Capt. C.P. PETER and 14 O.R. proceeded for Army.	A.T.A.
	19th		" " " 2nd Lt. W.H. SPACE M.C. D.C.M. and 12 O.R. d⁰ d⁰	
	20th		" " " " 17 O.R. d⁰ d⁰	
	21st		A and B Coys. moved to LA NEUVILLE. The Batt⁰ is now collected in one Camp. Major L.S.H. THOMAS M.C. and	A.T.A.
	22		Work on Camp Improvement. 2nd Lt J.L. RODERICK & 11 O.R. " "	A.T.A.
	23		" " " " " "	A.T.A.

Lt. W.E. DOWDING and 9 O.R. proceeded for Armies

19th Welsh Regt.   January 1919.

Army Form C. 2118.

WAR DIARY
or
INTELLIGENCE SUMMARY.

(Erase heading not required.)

Place	Date	Hour	Summary of Events and Information	Remarks and references to Appendices
LA NEUVILLE	23rd & 24th		Work on Camp Improvements, and Horse Standing continued.	
	25th		Do. do. 9. O.R. proceeded for demob to Lt. Col. R.B. HARKNESS Sgd. 008	008
	26th		Do. do. 13. O.R. " " and Capt. F.C. AUSTIN M.C. assumed comd.	
	27th		Do. do. 2nd Lt R.H. PUGH and 11. O.R. proceeded for Demob. M.C-M.M.	
	28th		Do. do. 9. O.R. " "	
	29th		Do. do. -------	
	30 & 31st		Do. do. 2nd Lt R.P. TRUEBLOOD and 9 O.R. " "	008

F.C. Austin Major
Comdg. 19.o Welch.

19th Field Regt

Army Form C. 2118.

WAR DIARY
or
INTELLIGENCE SUMMARY.

(Erase heading not required.)

February 1919

Instructions regarding War Diaries and Intelligence Summaries are contained in F. S. Regs., Part II. and the Staff Manual respectively. Title pages will be prepared in manuscript.

Place	Date	Hour	Summary of Events and Information	Remarks and references to Appendices
Ct NEUVILLE SOMME	1st		Week in Camp & an Hour Standing	
	2nd		Lt. S.M. WILLIAMS and 15. O.R. proceeded for Demob.	O.D.B.
	3rd		do do Lt. D.P. DAVIES " 11. O.R. "	
	4th & 5th		do do do do 12. O.R.	
			do do do do Hour Standing ready for occupation	O.D.B.
	6th		do do do do 10. O.R. proceeded for Demob.	
	7th		do do Visit of H.R.H. The Prince of Wales. H.R.H. inspected the Camp and spoke to many of the N.C.Os and men. All available Officers had the honour of being presented to the Prince who had a few cordial words for each. H.R.H. was accompanied by the Major General Comdg. the Divn. and his A.D.C. Capt Stuart Little.	
			10. O.R. proceeded for Demob.	O.D.B.
	8th		do do do do Lieut. S.H. ALLEN and 5. O.R. proceeded for Demob.	O.D.B.

Army Form C. 2118.

WAR DIARY
or
INTELLIGENCE SUMMARY.

(Erase heading not required.)

19th Welsh Regt February 1919

Place	Date	Hour	Summary of Events and Information	Remarks and references to Appendices
LA NEUVILLE SOMME.	9th		Do. do. do. Cleaning & painting vehicles – 11. O.R. proceeded for Demob". A load of Logging into the Camp of a large shed in Camp.	
	10th & 11th		Do. do. do. 11th The G.O.C. Div inspected the draft (2 Officers 86. O.R. details for transfer to the 2nd Army. (Rhine).	Appx A
	12th		Do. do. do.	
	13th		Do. do. do.	
	14th		Do. do. do.	
	15th		Do. do. do. Rd Inspection of Draft Appx 0.3. OR	
	16th		Do. do. do. 7. OR proceeded for Demob" 2. OR " " 3. OR " "	
	17th-18th		Do. do. do.	Appx B
	19th		Do. do. do.	
	20th		Do. do. do. 10. OR " "	
	21st		Do. do. do. 2. OR " "	Appx B

19th Welsh Regt

WAR DIARY
or
INTELLIGENCE SUMMARY. February 1919.

Army Form C. 2118.

Place	Date	Hour	Summary of Events and Information	Remarks and references to Appendices
LANEUVILLE	22nd		Do. do. do.	
SOMME.			"Peace Reported" 3. O.R. proceeded for Demob:	
	23rd & 24th		do. do. do. the M.M. awarded to 31152. C.Q.M.S. R.S Parrott. 31301. Sergt. F. Edwards. 31655. " E. Owen.	AAA.
	25th		do. do. do.	
	26th		do. do. do.	AAA.
	27th		do. do. do. Lieut. A.B. VAUGHAN and 38. O.R. proceeded for Demob. Adj/ Capt. D.M. MORGAN. Lieut. H.C. MILLER. 2nd Lt. F.J. PARCELL 2nd Lt. I.H.G. VAUGHAN and 96. O.R. proceeded to join 1/8th Welsh Regt. 1st Div. 2nd Army - Armies of Occupation.	AAA.
	28th		do. do. do. Extract from Lil 227. dated 18.2.19. Welsh Regt. 19th.B. "T/Capt. F.L. AUSTIN. M.C. to be act. Major whilst employed as 2nd in Comm? 4th Feb. 1919.	AAA.

O.D. Alant Capt Adj
Comdg. 19th Welsh Regt.

19th Welsh Regt

Army Form C. 2118.

Instructions regarding War Diaries and Intelligence Summaries are contained in F. S. Regs., Part II. and the Staff Manual respectively. Title pages will be prepared in manuscript.

WAR DIARY or INTELLIGENCE SUMMARY.
(Erase heading not required.)

March 1919. WO 40

Place	Date	Hour	Summary of Events and Information	Remarks and references to Appendices
LAMOTTILLE	1.		Lt. Colonel Major Austin proceeds on U.K. Special leave. 2/3/19 - 16/3/19 - Adj in comd.?	
CORBIE	2.		Sunday. Divine Service - Capt J. Perry Brown - Chaplain	
	3.		Bathing. Cleaning Camp. Cleaning unused Huts.	
	4.		Reading up Mob. Stores.	2 O.R. proceed for Demob.	App. I.
	5, 6		do.	movements —	
	7		do.	1 OR " "	
	8.		Stores handed to Class at GLISSY. Court of Inquiry into case of absence - held in camp. President Capt M.P. McDonough M.C.	App. II.
			3 OR proceeded for Demob	
	9, 10.			
	11, 12, 13, 14,		" " " "	12"
	15,			
	16, 17, 18		1 " " " "	
	19.		Lt. Col AUSTIN and 4. OR. "	App. III
	20, 21, 22.		Capt. T. LLEWELLYN returns from leave resumes comd.?	

40 7
2 sheets

Army Form C. 2118.

19th Worc'st Regt.   March 1919.

WAR DIARY
or
INTELLIGENCE SUMMARY.
(Erase heading not required.)

Instructions regarding War Diaries and Intelligence Summaries are contained in F. S. Regs., Part II. and the Staff Manual respectively. Title pages will be prepared in manuscript.

Place	Date	Hour	Summary of Events and Information	Remarks and references to Appendices
LA NEUVILLE	23, 24		—	
CORBIE	25th		Parade & Inspection of Centers.	
	26th		—	
	27th, 28th		Centres and Details move to Camp at BLANGY TRONVILLE joining the 114th Inf. Brig. Rifle Groups. Rear party left to clear camp.	OPS
BLANGY TRONVILLE	29th		11. OR proceeded for dispersal	
	30th		Party returned to 846 Camp to clear Brickfields.	
	31st		5. OR proceeded for dispersal. Rear Party returned to camp at BLANGY TRONVILLE.	OPS
			Camp at LA NEUVILLE cleared.	OPS

F.C. Marsh Lt. Col.
Comdg 19th Worc'st Regt

Confidential

H.Q. 115. 19TH (PIONEER) BATTALION — MAY 15 1919 — THE WELSH REGIMENT

38th Div

Herewith A.F. C2118
for the month of April, please

B J Dean Lt & A/Adjt
for O.C.
19th Welsh.

R 38
WL 41

WAR DIARY or INTELLIGENCE SUMMARY

Army Form C. 2118.

19th Welsh Regt.   April 1919

(Erase heading not required.)

Place	Date	Hour	Summary of Events and Information	Remarks and references to Appendices
BLANGY-TRONVILLE	1.2.3 5.	4 6.	Daily routine in Camp. –	
	7th		Participated in Divl. Route March. Lt. T.D. Walters proceeded to Eng. for Demob. Lt. R.M. Sampson " " "	BJJ
	8th		Unserviceable stores inspected by Ordnance Officer. Daily routine in Camp. –	
	9th		Parade & inspection of Cadre	
	10th		Lieut L. Edwards Capt. & Adjt. O.D. Black assumes proceeded to R.A.O.C. CALAIS the duties a 1 month's probation of Adjutant,	
	11th		Daily routine in Camp – Lt. W.H. Phillips proceeded to Eng. for Demob.	BJJ
	12th–16th		Daily routine in Camp. –	
	17th–19th		Stores inspected by C.O. Packing Cases constructed & all Stores packed.	
	20th		Daily routine in Camp. 2 O.R. (re-enlisted) proceeded to England on Furlough. 3 other	BJJ
	21st		Daily routine in Camp.	BJJ

Army Form C. 2118.

WAR DIARY
or
INTELLIGENCE SUMMARY.

19th Welsh   April 1919 (Cm.)

(Erase heading not required.)

Instructions regarding War Diaries and Intelligence Summaries are contained in F.S. Regs., Part II. and the Staff Manual respectively. Title pages will be prepared in manuscript.

Place	Date	Hour	Summary of Events and Information	Remarks and references to Appendices
BLANGY-TRONVILLE	22nd		Daily routine in Camp.	B.J.J.
	23rd	30*	Daily routine in Camp. 2 O.R. proceeded to Eng. for demob.	B.J.J.

H. Alexander Lt. Col.
Cmdg. 19th Bn The Welsh Regt.

[Stamp: HDQRS. 19TH. (PIONEER) BATTALION * THE WELSH REGIMENT * APR 30 1919]

www.ingramcontent.com/pod-product-compliance
Lightning Source LLC
Chambersburg PA
CBHW081538160426
43191CB00011B/1785